Robert's
Rules
of Writing

Robert's
Rules
of Writing

101
unconventional
lessons
every writer
needs to know

Robert Masello

WRITER'S DIGEST BOOKS
Cincinnati, Ohio
www.writersdigest.com

Visit our Web site at www.writersdigest.com for information on more resources for writers.

To receive a free weekly e-mail newsletter delivering tips and updates about writing and about Writer's Digest products, register directly at our Web site at http://newsletters.fwpublications.com.

09 08 07 06 05   5 4 3 2 1

Library of Congress Cataloging-in-Publication Data

Masello, Robert.
    Robert's rules of writing: 101 unconvential lessons every writer needs to know / by Robert Masello.
        p. cm.
    ISBN 1-58297-326-1 (pbk.: alk. paper)
1. Authorship. I. Title.

PN147.M427 2005
808'.02—dc22

                                                2004022324

Edited by Michelle Ruberg

Designed by Matthew DeRhodes

Cover designed by Matthew DeRhodes

Production coordinated by Robin Richie

F+W PUBLICATIONS, INC.

About the Author

Robert Masello is an award-winning journalist, successful television writer, and the author of fifteen previous books.

His articles, essays, and reviews have appeared often in such diverse publications as the *Los Angeles Times*, *New York Magazine*, *Newsday*, the *Washington Post*, *Redbook*, *Travel + Leisure*, *Harper's Bazaar*, *Glamour*, *Elle*, *TV Guide*, *Town & Country*, and the *Wilson Quarterly*.

He has published several novels—the most recent entitled *Vigil*—and many works of nonfiction, both here and abroad; his books have been translated into eight languages, ranging from Swedish to Korean. His look at the mysteries of the book business—*Writer Tells All: Insider Secrets to Getting Your Book Published*—was a *Los Angeles Times* best-seller.

In addition to various TV shows and specials, he has also written for many popular series that have aired on CBS, UPN, Fox, and Showtime.

An honors graduate of Princeton University, where he studied writing under Geoffrey Wolff and Robert Stone, he has since taught and lectured at the Columbia University Graduate School of Journalism, New York University, and Chapman University. He is currently the Visiting Lecturer in Literature at Claremont McKenna College.

Table of Contents

PREFACE

If you ask me, there are way too many books already out there on writing.

And I should know since I've written two of them.

By the time you're done buying all these books, you're too broke to pay the rent.

By the time you've carried them all home, you've dislocated something.

And by the time you're done reading them, you're too demoralized to write your own name.

So why another?

First of all, because I need the money. So there.

But on a higher note ... because none of those books does what this one will.

Those other books have other aims. They're either determined to unravel the most arcane rules of grammar and syntax for you ("a dependent clause can only take the subjective case when and if preceded by a dangling and/or perpendicular conjunction"), or else they're drowning you in a bubbly tide of inspirational gobbledygook. (Any simpleton who declares, "If you can talk, you can write!" should have a sock stuffed in his mouth.)

For the purposes of this book, I am just going to assume that you know all the basic principles already, and that you don't need a lecture on how to feel good about yourself.

I am going to assume that what you want is the stuff every professional writer learns from years of hard work. The straight, simple rules that address and smooth over the routine difficulties all writers face, whether they're working on a novel or a newspaper piece, a script or a memoir, a magazine article or an epic poem.

Some of these rules, let me warn you, are provocative, controversial, and counterintuitive. You may even want to duke it out with me over some of them (and that's okay, since you don't know where I live).

But you've just got to trust me—these rules have proven themselves over time to be of great, practical use to many writers of all stripes and all abilities. I know they have been to me.

Which is why I'm calling them— big surprise—*Robert's Rules of Writing*.

RULE 1.
Burn Your Journal

Just about every writing book I know says writing is a muscle you have to regularly exercise and keep in use, and that if you don't know what to write, you shouldn't let that stop you. You should just start keeping a journal and writing down, at random, all your thoughts and ideas.

In my book—this one to be exact—that's an immense waste of time and paper. The only muscle you'll exercise by keeping a journal is your hand, and for that you'd be better off jumping rope.

If you feel like keeping a journal—that neither you nor anyone else on earth will ever want to read—be my guest. But if you want to write something that may eventually see the light of day, that a magazine might buy or a publisher publish, then you'll have to knock off the journaling and do the grunt work that real writing requires.

Nine out of ten struggling writers get stuck right there. Instead of confronting all the very real problems that any book, article, or short story poses, they retreat to their journals, on the theory that they're working out their literary muscles, loosening up their artistic tendons, free-associating their way to fresh ideas.

All they're really doing is keeping the manufacturers of those fancy blank books, the ones that uselessly clutter up the shelves at your local bookstores, in business.

Writing in a journal is just a stall, a waiting game, a way to tell yourself that you're working when you're not, that you're doing something of value when you're just using up paper, that you're a writer when in fact you're just going through the motions of one. *Look at me! I have blank paper in front of me—and now I'm filling it, with words!*

Anyone can do that. Anytime.

The hard part of writing isn't scribbling words on a page. The hard part is scribbling words that *mean* something, that make sense, that build a narrative or lay out an argument, that construct a scene or articulate a position. It's not about how many pages you can cover with ink in a day. In some cases, a good day's work might be a couple of paragraphs. But if those two paragraphs are right, then they're a lot more valuable than ten or twenty pages of idle burbling.

Writing takes deliberation and thought, craft and commitment.

If you're serious about writing, burn the journal and get to work.

Get a Pen Pal.
RULE 2.

But I don't want you to think I'm too hard-hearted.

I know what it's like to be stuck, to have the urgent *desire* to write, but nothing particular to say just now. That's usually when those blasted journals come out.

But try this. Instead of writing the stream-of-consciousness twaddle that generally fills those blank pages, do this instead—write a letter to a friend.

Writing has to have a purpose; it's meant to communicate something to someone, and if you're not ready to write for the general public—many times we're not—then try writing for a very specific audience—one you know will be happy to hear from you. (People are so astonished to get letters these days, you might want to warn them that one is on the way.) If you must, you could even make it an e-mail, but there's something about the ephemerality of e-mails that virtually cries out for sloppiness and imprecision. A good, old-fashioned letter, on paper, will require you to think before you write, will permit you to edit and revise and amend.

All the things, in other words, that honest-to-God writing makes you do!

It'll also put you in touch with a lot of important things. For one, your ideal audience. Much of the time, writers are stuck because they can't figure out who they're writing for, or because they've started imagining their audience as an indifferent, even hostile, crowd—a bunch of critics just waiting to take a shot at them. Writing to a friend will remind you that there are nice folks out there, folks you like and who like you back, who would be only too happy to hear what you have to say.

Writing a letter can also remind you, in case you'd forgotten, what it is that you actually have to say.

Look and see what flows from your flying fingertips or your scrawling pen. Are you ranting about the next-door neighbors? Are you seeking comfort for a broken heart? Are you telling a funny story about the perfectly awful job interview you just went on? Whatever it is, *that's* what you're thinking about, *that's* what's on your mind. And, if you wanted to, that's what you could be writing about for others, too—the broken-heart story might be right for a women's magazine, the dismal job interview could work as a humor piece for the local paper, the rotten neighbors could be characters in a screenplay.

But because you're writing now with a purpose and a person in mind—instead of just sprawling all over a journal—you're paying attention, the way you should, to everything from pace to clarity. You're writing to interest and even entertain the friend who's going to receive this letter in a few days. And, secretly, you're looking forward to the reaction your words are going to get.

However limited, writing a letter is a form of publication. Next time you can go after a bigger crowd.

RULE 3.

Throw Out

How many times,
when you're telling a story, do you stop
dead to search for a bigger, better, or more impressive word
than the one you were just about to utter?

Unless you were planning on losing your audience, probably
not very often.

So why do it when you're writing?

The best writing is the writing that flows naturally,
without impediment or hesitation, from the mind of the
writer. It's writing that appears to have come effortlessly
(however much effort actually went into it behind the scenes).
It's writing that sounds like its author—you—and that uses your
rhythm, your sensibility, and your vocabulary.

The minute you pick up a thesaurus, you've muddied the
waters. Into the clear running stream of your prose, you've
introduced a foreign agent. Nothing sticks out in a piece of
prose like the words you've plucked from those long lists of
synonyms, each one more obscure than its predecessor.

Thesaurus words are words you would never use on your own;
the fact that you had to resort to the thesaurus just to find them
proves it. They aren't words that come readily to your mind
or rest comfortably in your working vocabulary. Suddenly, you
start sounding like William F. Buckley—and unless you're
William F. Buckley, that's not a good thing. (Even if you are,
it's debatable.) It's as if you've swapped your customary Hawaiian

Your Thesaurus.

shirts and shorts for a three-piece suit and a watch fob. If you think people won't notice, think again.

The voice you write in is the voice your reader hears and, ideally, grows to trust.

It's the voice the reader becomes accustomed to, the one that makes a sort of pact between the two of you. When you stop writing with your own words—the words you would or could summon up on your own—you break that pact and you propel the reader out of your world and straight into Mr. Roget's. It's no different than if you were writing fiction and you put into a character's mouth words the character could never have called up or spoken on his own. If you wrote about a farmhand and had him talking like a college professor, or a cultivated diplomat sounding like a stevedore, you'd be shaking your reader's belief not only in the character but in the entire fictional world the character inhabits.

Whatever it is you want to say in your work, find a way to say it not in words you've borrowed for this special occasion but in words you already own. Those are the words your readers will find the most convincing.

RULE 4:
Zip the Lip:

Ever notice how, when an interviewer asks an author about his next project, the author gets very evasive? "Oh, I'm just noodling with a couple of things right now," or, "Well, I hate to jinx anything by talking about it too soon ... "

Take an important cue from this.

Professional writers know that the more you talk about something you're planning to write, the less likely it is that you'll ever write it.

A book is like a hydraulic engine, and the more you talk about it, the more you let out the power that's needed to make the thing run. All the energy that should be going back into the book is being squandered in talk and dissipated in the air.

If people ask what you're up to these days, it's perfectly all right to say you're working on a book. A murder mystery, a biography, a memoir of your curious years as an enforcer for the mob. If you try to dodge the question altogether, they'll think you're being snooty.

But if you talk too much, you'll get into trouble. Either you'll start going on about the subject of your book until your friends are bored to tears or, and this is even more dangerous, you'll go on about it until you begin to get bored yourself. There's nothing like hearing your story told over and over again to take the zest out of it, for you and everybody else.

In every book you write, there will be things you discover only along the way, points you suddenly want to make, themes that slowly emerge, stories that take surprising turns. But the place to discover these things is on the page, as you write, not at some cocktail party where the best you can do is jot something down on a napkin and hope, when you fish the darn thing out of your pocket the next morning, that it isn't hopelessly smudged and illegible.

Carry the book you're writing in your imagination,
but keep your mouth closed.

That way, nothing that belongs to the book will escape—no image will fade from overexposure, no dialogue will become rote, and no idea will lose its full impact.

Sealed in its original container—your head—
your work will retain all its freshness and flavor.

RULE 5.

Call Out the Thought Police.

If there's one question successful writers get asked at virtually every public event they attend, it's "Where do you get your ideas?"—as if they could tell you, "Oh, yeah, there's this great little shop on the corner of Lexington and Twenty-Third. But go early, because the fresh ideas are gone by ten."

Would that there were such a shop. The line would be around the block.

No, the best place to get ideas—for articles, essays, books, stories, scripts—is much closer to home than that. It's your own head, if only you'll learn to pay proper attention to what's going on in there.

Sure, you can sit down with a legal pad in your lap, shut your eyes, press your hands to your temples, and bid the ideas to come. But that probably works as well as guessing the right lottery numbers. Pressing hard, for something as ephemeral as an idea, is as fruitless as it is exhausting.

Meanwhile, all day long, every day, great notions are flowing right by you, but just under your radar. Where are they? What are they? They're in the thoughts you're thinking as you drive to work or as you sit on the bus observing your fellow passengers. They're crossing your mind while you have dinner with friends and somebody says something that makes you laugh. They're in the tub with you, as you lie back with your head on the cold porcelain rim and wonder what your colleague really meant by that weird remark at work.

All day long, like a radio that's never turned off, your mind is broadcasting your interests, your obsessions, your worries, your fears, your deepest concerns, and these are the raw materials from which you will build your most effective work. They're the things that please and plague you, trouble and tempt you, the things that get your sympathies engaged, your temper aroused, your sense of humor tickled. But because you're doing something else at the time—because you're not actually in the working mode—you're not paying attention, and you're not giving these thoughts their due.

In fact, half the time you're trying to banish these thoughts—so what if the third girlfriend in a row has just broken up with you for no reason you can discern? You tell yourself to forget about it and think about something more constructive. Like your stock portfolio. But your thoughts, undoubtedly, keep returning to that sore point. What is it, you wonder, that women really want? Is it even remotely possible that you are doing something wrong? Should you *not* have suggested that she throw out everything in her closet and replace it all with those catalog items you'd helpfully flagged with colorful Post-it notes? Was that … insensitive?

Here's your material, here's your mother lode. Here's something you feel strongly about, even if your chief emotion is confusion. And this is where you will find your most successful stories and essays. When you sit at your computer, hell-bent on coming up with some important concept, you are asking for trouble; before you know it, you will be jotting down big themes like "man's inhumanity to man" or intractable problems like the first world's reluctance to forgive third world debt. That's all fine if you're on the editorial staff of some newspaper, but for the rest of us, that kind of material is dead on arrival. Killed by noble intentions.

Meanwhile, the stuff you scorn, the quotidian chaff your mind keeps turning over and over, is where your fortune lies. Let the big themes emerge, if they will, from the everyday questions, the Sturm und Drang of your daily existence, from the stuff with which you are, for good or ill, consumed. Pay attention to what's playing in your head at any old time of the day, and don't be so quick to dismiss it. You could be throwing out the best work you'd ever have done.

RULE 6.
Don't Overinflate the Balloon.

Attuning your antenna to the mundane is also a good way to ward off another affliction. The problem is an insidious one, and its seeds are usually sown in high school when a teacher innocently asks, "And what does the white whale really stand for?" or, "Why does Holden Caulfield dream of standing in a field? And why, specifically, *rye*?"

The disease is called "symbolitis," and the farther down that road you go, the more confused you and your writing will become.

When we study Literature—and I mean that with the capital L— we learn to comb over the text with a magnifying glass, looking for everything from circular motifs in *Madame Bovary* to religious iconography in Steinbeck. We're looking at everything on the page to see what else it might mean *off* the page. Is it by chance, or design, that a snake is seen in the swimming hole? Does the protagonist have the initials J.C.—as in Jesus Christ—for a reason? Does the scarlet letter have to be red? Before you know it, you start to think that that's how writers write—that they start out with some elaborate blueprint of mystical clues and meanings they cleverly embed and embroider in a narrative expressly designed to carry their weight—when in fact they seldom do anything of the kind.

Writers write a story, not a theme. They write about things, not symbols, characters, icons. They write dialogue, not polemics. (At least the good ones do.)

If symbols and themes emerge from the text, they only do so later on, and in most cases without the author even having been aware of them at the time she was writing. I know this is heresy in the eyes of the academic establishment, which sustains itself by foraging for such truffles, but if you ask me, much of what passes for literary analysis is about as reliable as astrology and reveals a deep incomprehension of the creative act. If you actually set out with a symbolic and/or thematic edifice in mind, then you might as well become an architect instead of an author. A book is not an Erector set.

And it isn't an enemy code, either, which you'd need the Enigma Machine to decipher. Without getting too fundamentalist about it, it's the words, in black ink, on the white page. That's what you as a reader read, and that's what you as an author write. If you let things be what they are, and write about them truthfully, then you've done your job. Deliberately trying to invest these things with metameanings is the surest route to madness; the more you inflate your writing, the sooner it will pop like a great big empty balloon.

RULE 7. Skip the Starbucks.

For many writers, nothing goes better with a laptop than a double café mocha at the closest Starbucks. At the rate they're opening, there may soon be one in your own living room—but for now we'll assume you still have to leave the house.

Which is largely the point.

The theory behind the Starbucks School of Writing, to which countless aspiring writers subscribe, is simple—you'll do your best and most concentrated work when you're out of the house and losing yourself in a crowded café, surrounded by deafening cappuccino machines, swinging doors, and tiny tables jammed with equally striving strangers.

Of course, the theory is wrong—what you really get out of a trip to Starbucks is a nice caffeine buzz and the heady impression that you've been working when in fact you haven't.

Starbucks is where writers who want to be *seen* in the act of creation go, who treat writing as if it were some kind of performance art. They want to be admired, they want to be soothed by the ambient noise and the occasional glance from an attractive patron. They want to be asked, "What are you working on?" so they can sit back and talk about it.

Or scowl importantly and say, "Sorry, I can't be disturbed right now."

When, if they really and truly wanted to be undisturbed, they'd stay home in the first place, make a cup of Folgers instant (for about a nickel), and concentrate.

I know the problem; I know the temptation. Nobody wants to lock himself up in a room and write. Neither do I. Most days I trudge into my office like a guy on a chain gang. It's lonely in there—even the dog goes downstairs. And it's scary—I know I'll have no one to amuse me but me, and what if I can't think of anything all that good? Sometimes, at a total loss, I just stare out the window at the guy in the apartment across the way; he's got a plasma-screen TV the size of a picnic table, but lately, I've noticed, he's taken to lowering his blinds.

Still, it's in my own little office that the actual writing gets done.

In solitude. In silence. With no cappuccino machine anywhere in sight.

And no living witnesses to the act of creation.

When I do go to Starbucks, it's to reward myself for doing a good day's work.

Never mistake Starbucks for your office— and leave the laptop home.

RULE 8.
Take the Prozac.

Legend has it that once, long ago, in a land far away, there was a writer who wasn't depressed.

But don't believe it.

Writing, in case you haven't yet noticed, can be a very depressing occupation. You have to sit alone in a room, for hours on end, just brooding. If you weren't depressed when you started, trust me—you will be by the time you're done.

Now, a lot of people are under the impression that if they mess with their mood, they'll also mess with their art. Keats was depressed, Plath was depressed, Virginia Woolf was depressed, Hemingway was depressed, Styron was (still is?) depressed. Bleakness of spirit is just the price you pay for artistic fulfillment and creativity. Right?

Wrong.

Depression can be crippling, making you unable even to sit at the keyboard or lift the pen, or it can be milder and chronic—what's called dysthymia—but either way, it's not helping your art, it's hurting it. It's sapping your confidence, disturbing your sleep, laying waste to your energy reserves. It's not the wellspring of your genius and creativity, it's the sump pump sucking your happiness and productivity down the drain. True, lots of writers, for time immemorial, have managed to work through it, but at what a terrible cost, to themselves and to the people who have had to eat cereal with them in the morning.

Nor is it all that picturesque. I know, it's easy to believe you have to suffer for your art. Aren't creative types supposed to wear a lot of black and fly into a temper now and then? Aren't they duty bound to be prickly and difficult? Not really. While it's a commonly held impression of the artistic temperament, I defy you to show me the manual that demands it.

So take the Prozac, the Zoloft, whatever your medical professional may have prescribed. Or just get out and see some friends. Catch a movie. Go to a ball game. Don't fear, as many writers do, that if you start having some fun and enjoying yourself, you'll somehow take away from your art. You won't. Your work will get better, you'll produce even more of it, and your loved ones won't be quite so sorely tempted to pack their bags and leave you in the dead of night.

Of all the ways writers find to waste time, waiting for the muse to show up has to be the most common, and fruitless, of them all.

So if you're waiting for her, too, stop it right now.

RULE 9. Lose the Muse.

The muse—the embodiment of inspiration, usually portrayed as a comely woman loosely draped in a diaphanous gown—is what every writer longs for. Once she appears, you're supposed to be able to write effortlessly, at the height of your powers, with an unequaled command and energy and zest.

Must be nice.

As anyone who actually writes on a regular basis can attest, the muse is a very unreliable creature. Sometimes she shows up at noon, raring to go; sometimes she shows up at midnight, just when you're ready to call it a day. And sometimes, no matter how many times you put out an SOS, she doesn't appear at all. She doesn't return your calls, she doesn't come to your door (that you've left conveniently unlocked); she's simply missing in action. Gone without a trace. No forwarding address.

Which is why you cannot build your writing life around her.

Sometimes you'll feel inspired when you sit down to write—and sometimes you won't. That's just the way it is. But sit down you must, and write you will, and if there's one thing every writer learns over time, it's this: The muse is most effectively summoned by the clicking of your keyboard or the scratching of your pen. Once you stop worrying about where she is, and focus instead on doing the work at hand, she is most likely to put in a surprise appearance. Most of the time, you'll be so absorbed in your work that you won't even notice when she's slipped into the room. You'll just keep on writing, your head down, your fingers flying, and only when you finish, and sit back with satisfaction to read over what you've done, will it dawn on you that she was there, after all. The evidence is all right there, on the pages in front of you.

The muse may come and go at will,

silent and unseen, a woman of unpredictable habits and mysterious ways.

But there is one thing every writer does get to know about her over time:

She is irresistibly drawn to the aroma of hard work.

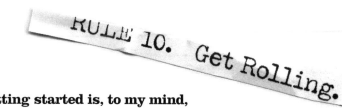

RULE 10. Get Rolling.

Getting started is, to my mind, the worst part of a writer's work. Every day it's like sitting down in a car that's been left outside in a snow-storm for three days and trying to get the engine to turn over. Press on the gas too gently and the car won't start, press on it too hard and you flood the engine. It's a tricky maneuver and no way to start work.

All through the ages, writers have been looking for ways to avoid this problem. Ernest Hemingway made it a practice to stop writing somewhere in the middle of a passage that was going well. His theory was that he could then jump right into that section the next day, pick up the momentum where he'd left off, and keep right on rolling into the virgin territory beyond. The car engine, in his case, was always warm that way.

The English novelist Anthony Trollope was a meticulous craftsman who had his daily quota and stuck to it religiously. Every day he produced, I think it was, 2,000 words, and if 1,950 of them completed the novel he was working on, then the following 50 were applied to the next book he'd had in mind. For him, the car apparently started every time, without fail, so he hardly needed a method at all.

Philip Roth, according to an interview I once read, writes a couple of pages a day, then spends the next day revising the last page or so, before plowing on from there. A slower way to start, but if it works for Roth …

Personally, I've tried 'em all. Hemingway's approach is a good idea, but I found it very hard to make myself abandon work just when things were going well. If the writing was really flowing, there was no way I was going to staunch or impede it in any way—I wanted the aqueduct to remain wide open. The time or two I did try stopping in midstream and returning the next day, it was never quite the same. I always felt it would have been better if I'd stayed in the flow, as it were, the day before. But that's me. (And it's all part of a general perception I sadly cling to, that under slightly different circumstances—another time, another place, a firmer chair—I would be writing much better than I do. Again, not your problem.)

One thing I do know, and recommend, is that you give some serious thought to where you will be picking up your work the next time you sit down. Often, after finishing up a day's work, I've had some vague notion, an idea of where I'd start up again, but then I've made the fatal mistake of not jotting down any rudimentary notes or clues. I was so sure I'd remember it all the next day. Well, I didn't, and you might not, either. And even if you do have some faint glimmering, you'll remain convinced that there's still something missing, that you had a much better, fuller, more intriguing idea the previous day, and you'll then squander an hour kicking yourself for not being able to recall it.

Trust me, though—you didn't have a better idea. And the way to prove it is to start regularly making a few notes to yourself as soon as you're done writing for the day. Leave yourself some indication as to where, to the best of your knowledge, the narrative is supposed to go next. Do it before you get up from your desk, do it before you turn out the light and go to sleep, but do it, one way or the other. That way you'll have something to look at the next morning, over the rim of your coffee cup, as you contemplate the fearful plunge back into your manuscript.

RULE 11.
Let the Well Refill

Still, there will
be times, long dark nights of the
soul, when you don't know where your writing
is going. When you're not sure what befalls your hero next,
or you're unclear on how to develop your argument further,
or you feel that your article is missing some important research
element—but you're just not quite sure what it is.

And while sticking with it, staying on your work schedule,
sitting down at your desk at the same time every day is generally
the best way to break the blockade, there are times, I will concede,
when even that is not going to work.

At those times, take a break.

Henry James described it as letting "the well of unconscious
cerebration" refill (but then, Henry James would put it that
way, wouldn't he?). Still, the analogy is a good one. All your
ideas come from deep inside you, from the well of what you
think and feel and know and fear and love, and that well can
occasionally become occluded, or it can seem (even though
it hasn't really—it never does) to have gone dry.

By focusing your energies elsewhere for a little while,

you can give the well some time to replenish itself;

this, for instance, would be a very good
time to clean out the garage, make
those new curtains for the dining room,
or reconnect with some old friends.

As the level of the well water rises, so,
too, does the ease with which you'll be able
to fill your humble bucket. (Enough of this
metaphor, I swear.)

It's also a matter of perspective.
Sometimes you are simply so close to your
work, so deeply enmeshed in its gears, that
you can't see what's gumming things up. You
have to step back, and step away, in order to
see where the problem lies. It could be something as simple as a false plot turn, one that
sent you careening off in the wrong direction,
or it could be something as major as a loss
of faith in the project (which I'll get to in
greater detail shortly). Whatever it is, a short
break can give you the time and distance
necessary to assess the difficulties and ideally
address them. Sometimes it's a quick fix, and sometimes—
though you will shrink from it—the required repairs are
extensive. If it's the latter, just roll up your sleeves and get
to it. The longer you wait, or try to come up with some
smaller, simpler way around what is the obvious, festering
problem, the more time and energy you will ultimately waste.

The uglier the job, the better it is to tackle it straightaway.
Why postpone the inevitable?

RULE 12. Tell, Don't Show.

"Isn't that supposed to be the other way around?" you may ask.

Not always.

Writers have been hearing about the importance of "showing" for so long that they've begun to forget the value of "telling"— of exposition, of summary, of omniscient narration.

If you've got something *worth* showing, then by all means show it. If it's a dramatic action, let us see it happen. If it's a scintillating exchange of dialogue, then let us hear it, every word.

But don't be afraid to tell us things, too. Don't be afraid to tell us, with all your powers of description and even a bit of attitude, about an atmosphere, a landscape, about what's going on in a character's mind or in the larger world of your story. Don't be afraid to enter into your tale, to limn its greater dimensions and suggest its meanings. It was good enough for Dickens, who told us right off the bat in *A Tale of Two Cities*, that "It was the best of times, it was the worst of times," or who opened *Bleak House* with an unforgettable description of the fog descending on Chancery Court—the fog that would seem to enfold and befuddle and frustrate all the characters later to be drawn into the irresolvable case of Jarndyce vs. Jarndyce.

Don't feel you have to show us the things we don't actually need to see, either. If your heroine gets up in the morning and gets ready for work, we don't need to see her take a shower, brush her teeth, put on her shoes, make coffee, and butter her toast. We just need to know she's on her way to work. Elmore Leonard, a master of pacing, once said he keeps his books moving briskly along by leaving out all the parts readers don't want to read.

The same goes for nonfiction. If you're writing a travel piece, you don't need to take us along every step of the way; you can jump straight from one port of call to the next. If it's a personality profile, feel free to give us a general impression of your interview subject; we don't need to hear every single word or see every single action he performs. Use a fine brush when you have to, but take some broad strokes, too. Life is short, and so is the attention span of most magazine readers.

The omniscient voice, the one that knows everything and sees into the minds of all, is the voice that *tells*. But in so doing, it's the most intimate, the most powerful, and the most all-embracing voice imaginable. It's the voice you use, as an author, to whisper directly into your reader's ear, to offer a greater sense of your purpose, your design, and your own point of view. It's a chance to play God, and since those come along so seldom, it'd be a shame to pass up even one.

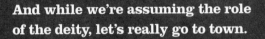

**And while we're assuming the role
of the deity, let's really go to town.**

Anytime you confront the blank page,
you're confronting a void, an emptiness
you are about to fill. In so doing, you are about to bring
into existence a whole new world—even if that world is going
to be so small as to fit into a six-hundred-word essay or as
large as *The Lord of the Rings*. Everything you put into it will be a
part of that world, and everything you leave out will remain
outside of it. Yes, we the readers will bring to it all sorts of
previously acquired knowledge, assumptions, information—
Stephen Crane could assume we'd already heard of the Civil
War before we opened *The Red Badge of Courage*—but a well-
wrought narrative establishes its own universe, in which we
suspend (for the time being) what we already know, as well as
accept the limitations and, most notably, the perspective of
the world we are presently inhabiting.

We must also, however, be able to accept the rules and regulations of that world. We must find them credible and, above
all, consistent. Does that mean you can't write a vampire novel
in which the vampire gets around, untroubled, in the daylight?
Or a movie like *Groundhog Day*, in which the hero keeps waking
up and reliving the same day of his life until he somehow manages to get things right? Of course not. You can create any
wild, surreal, imaginary world you want, where white rabbits
lead proper young ladies down holes in the ground, where
budding wizards study sorcery in secret academies, where a

magical ring holds the power of world dominion, but whatever world you create, you are bound, as is your reader, by the logical parameters of that world. Whatever rules you set up—that dead people can be seen by one boy but no one else, that the monster will heed only his creator's commands, that the evil hotel needs to corrupt a human agent to feed its bloody needs—you are restricted by those same rules, and if you break them, you do so at your peril. There's a bond of trust between you, the writer, and your readers. The reader is saying, "Take my hand, lead me anywhere you want, but I'm counting on you to keep me informed of how things work in this world." And you, in turn, are saying to your reader, "Come on along, don't sweat it, I'll show you the ropes. You may get a few surprises and scares along the way, but nothing that happens will break with anything you've been promised so far. If my vampire, who's been walking in the sunlight with no problem in chapter one, suddenly explodes into flame in chapter two, I'll at least account for it somehow." (Insufficient sunblock?) Once too many rules get broken, or even bent, the reader will begin to lose confidence in the story. After all, if anything can happen, at any time, then nothing can really matter, ever.

Einstein,

in search of a unified theory, famously insisted that "God does not play dice with the universe." Nor can you with yours.

RULE 14. Stop Reading.

Impossible, you may say. Writers read all the time—and if they don't, they're not really writers.

I would not argue with that.

But I would say that once you've embarked on a writing project,

the last thing you want to do is start filling your head with other people's prose,

with their characters, their dialogue, with another writer's way of looking at things, or describing them.

What you're trying to preserve, what you're trying to protect, is your own voice and your own approach. I know that when I was in high school, and I had to write a paper on Herman Melville and *Moby-Dick*, I produced a paper that read like it had been written by a teenage Melville himself, filled with portentous prose, vague pronouncements, and syntax so elaborate that even I could not have unscrambled it. I was under the spell of a master, and I hadn't managed to shake myself out of it.

Doing your own work now, you want to create your own spell, and that's hard enough to do without being under someone else's. In fact, the better the writer you might be reading, the more danger you're in. The style will be just that much more seductive, the work itself more compelling. You'll settle down in your easy chair, convinced that reading just a few more chapters will do you no harm, but chances are you'll keep

on reading—reading is always so much easier than writing—
and your own work will begin to shift, in its structure, its prose
rhythm, even its ideas.

Reading bad stuff, though you're less likely to emulate it,
has its own dangers, of course. You can pick up some nasty
habits, and your standards can start to fall without you even
noticing it. Cheap, brassy prose ceases to clang in your ear.
(When I began to write articles for *New York Magazine*, I had
to stop writing their ad copy, which I'd also been doing; though
I missed the income, I knew that writing stuff like, "Wow! That's
a savings of 33 percent off the newsstand cost!" was interfering
with my higher calling.)

Still, you probably can't go cold turkey and stop reading
altogether—I know, I've tried. But as a rule of thumb, try not to
read anything too close to what you're working on. In other
words, when writing a sensitive novel, you might want to read
only nonfiction, and even then only nonfiction well removed
from your subject matter. For instance, if I'm writing fiction,
that's when I read a big fat biography. Or else I just resort to
newspapers and magazines. The deeper I am into a big project—
novel, screenplay, feature piece—the more I turn to periodicals
to get my reading fix. You can read a few articles, finish them in
one brief sitting, and toss the paper or magazine aside. There's
very little chance of you being taken away from your own work
for too long, or too irresistibly. You'll be away just long enough
to satisfy your craving for new and other words, and refreshed
enough to throw yourself back, reinvigorated, into the creation
of your own magnum opus.

RULE 15.

Wave Good-bye

I have a writer friend who spends more time trying to catch the next publishing wave than he does actually writing anything. So consumed is he with whether the horror market is up or down, the thriller market saturated, the romance shelves stocked or barren, that he seldom gets around to figuring out what it is he really wants to write himself. He's a publishing speculator more than he is an active participant. And his system—trying to write sci-fi when that appears to be making a resurgence, or hacking out a Mary Higgins Clark–style book when domestic mysteries seem to be popular— has been an utter bust.

Not that that keeps him from trying.

The thing about waves, in publishing and in popular taste, is that by the time you spot one, it's invariably too late to catch it. So don't even try.

Given that it takes roughly nine months, at best, to get a finished book out into the marketplace, and that's not counting the time it would actually take to *write* such a book in the first place, you can see that there's little point in trying to assess and extrapolate anything, with certainty, from the current situation. Right around the time you drag yourself, and your project, across the finish line, you will look up to see that everything has changed (What? Hot pants are back? Again?) while you were hunkered down in your lonely bunker.

Not to mention the more critical problem, which is that nobody's good at everything. Henry James wanted to be a playwright, but that just wasn't his forte. (Of course, I know many people who, having struggled through *The Golden Bowl* in college, would claim that novels weren't either.) When you try to write the kind of material that you don't really respond to yourself— whether it's a black-humor piece for a magazine, a disaster-flick screenplay, a coming-of-age novel—you've got to remember that you're up against a thousand other writers who really *do* like that particular kind of stuff and who, as a result, are bound to do it a lot better than you.

And as for that vast theoretical marketplace, the one where one genre is up and another one down, keep in mind that the good stuff always finds its way. Just because publishers may not be as interested in military hardware thrillers as they once were doesn't mean they've lost interest altogether. And just because the Hollywood studios say they don't want to see sports-oriented scripts anymore doesn't mean the right one won't change their minds. (Before Sylvester Stallone wrote *Rocky*, boxing movies were anathema.) If it's done with enough conviction and style and narrative drive, there's a market out there for nearly anything. Write it right and your audience will find you.

RULE 16.
Write What You Read

Take a look at your bedside table and tell me what— besides the alarm clock and the Kleenex box —**is sitting there.**

A book, perhaps?

If so, what kind of book? (And don't lie.)

Is it a romance novel? A techno-thriller? A sci-fi epic?

Chances are, whatever kind of book is sitting on your bedside table is the kind of book you should be writing yourself.

Why?

Because, clearly, that's what you most enjoy. That's the kind of book you curl up with at the end of the day for pure pleasure. And the kind of book you most enjoy is the kind of book you will stand the best chance of writing well yourself.

Successful writing is writing done with conviction. It's writing in which the author was truly invested. If what you like is spy stories, that's fine; no reason to be ashamed, and even less reason to try to write the kind of mainstream literary novel (a deeply revealing portrait of middle-aged anomie in America's heartland, or whatever) that you would never pick up yourself.

If you wouldn't read it, you will not be able to write it.

By writing the sort of thing you enjoy reading, you give your-self another advantage, too—especially when you're starting out. Instead of venturing into uncharted territory, you're treading familiar ground, where you instinctively know the landscape, the landmarks, the most successful routes. Even if you couldn't articulate these things, you know them in your bones, just from having been there so many times before. And when you write, you'll be aware, pretty soon, if you have veered from the path. You'll also know how to get back on it.

Every kind of writing has its own conventions, from the climactic love scene in a romance novel to the shoot-out in a Western. You know what you would expect from such a book, and so you know, too, what your readers will expect from yours. Put that knowledge and expertise to use. Write what you would want to find on your own bedside table, and there's a very good chance you'll have written something that lots of other people will want to put on theirs.

RULE 17. Make 'Em Worry.

If there's one thing you want your readers to do, it's worry.

Huh? Doesn't everyone hate to worry?

Not when it comes to reading. Worry is what keeps people turning the pages. Will your characters survive? Will they prevail? Will they overcome all the obstacles you throw in their way and, in the end, get what they want? Your mission is to keep your readers guessing.

Imagine if you wrote a story in which everybody started out knowing just what he wanted, and then in short order got it. What kind of story would that be? How would it get readers involved? Who would it leave them to root for? And how on earth would you manage to fill enough pages to make a story, much less a book, out of it?

No, the essence of any story is obstacles and—yes, you've heard this a million times—*conflict*. The worst thing you can do for your characters is give them an easy time of it. If they're meant to be lovers, make sure they're already engaged to other people. If your hero needs to make a fortune, make sure he loses one first.

If he needs to get somewhere, make sure the road is washed out and there's an angry trucker on his tail. Your readers want to see, even savor, the struggle; they want to see the odds overcome, the hurdles jumped, the victories won. Imagine if Inman, the hero of *Cold Mountain*, had just decided, "Okay, I've had it with this war," turned around, and gone home, unimpeded, to his sweetheart. Awfully short book, awfully short movie (though *that* would have been a blessing to us all).

Does that mean your story has to end happily?

Absolutely not. Just ask Madame Bovary or Anna Karenina.

Heck, even a good newspaper story makes us worry some. I just read a story in the local paper about a grave miscarriage of justice, another of those juries that just can't see straight. I knew from the headline that it was a mistrial, but I read on to find out what had derailed the prosecution's case and to hear whether or not the malefactors (caught on a videotape of their own making) would be retried or escape unscathed. An editorial, in the same issue of the paper, had me worried about global warming and the holes in the ozone layer. What, short of throwing away my aerosol cans, I could do about it was unclear, but it did feel right to worry for at least a few minutes.

In art, as in life,
things don't always work out for the best.

But in art, just as in life, what makes things interesting
and memorable is how events play out.

How do people play the hand that's dealt them? Do they
fold, or do they bluff? Do they conserve what they have left,
or do they raise the ante? It doesn't matter if you're writing a
novel, a memoir, or an exposé—you want to keep your audience
wondering how things will turn out, worrying that they won't
go well, and unable to stop reading until they've found out
for themselves.

RULE 18.

Every writer has at least one of these: The great idea that got away. The brilliant story twist that came in a flash and departed just as quickly. The beautiful turn of phrase that would have perfectly capped the epic poem. The shocking act break that would have left the audience breathless.

All lost, for want of ... what?

A pad? A pen? Okay, that's easy enough to remedy. Any writer worth his ink learns to carry something around with him to record his thoughts and inspirations. (Remember that journal, mentioned earlier, that I recommended you burn? If you didn't do that yet, you can use it for this instead.) Balzac made notes wherever he went, and *The Human Comedy*, all thirty-eight volumes of it, is stuffed with the material he relentlessly accumulated every day.

But the larger problem remains—training yourself to do the same thing. I know, I know, you *think* you'll remember all the good ideas that cross your brainpan. An intriguing thought will come to you, and you'll smile and tuck it away in a mental file folder, which you'll then dutifully deposit in the "Short-Term Memory" vault of your cerebral cortex.

Only, God help you when you go to retrieve it.

Even in a matter of hours, it will be gone. Look all you want, but all you'll remember is a fragment, a tantalizing piece of the amazing, and startlingly original, whole. And that taste—worse than forgetting the thing in its entirety—will torment you like a bad commercial jingle you can't get out of your head.

Memo Yourself.

How much better would it have been to have simply jotted down a note or two at the time you first had this breathtaking idea?

My mother, a writer herself, always slept with a pad and pen on her bedside table, and once, in the dead of night, she had a dream of the perfect locked-room mystery story. A man found murdered, alone, in a third-floor room, locked from the inside. The only window, firmly closed, had no balcony, no fire escape, and there was no rope hanging from its sill, no footprints in the soil below it. When she woke up and remembered scrawling down the solution to the mystery, she grabbed the pad and eagerly read, in her sleepy handwriting, "The tree did it!"

Though the motive was still missing, apparently it was the tree outside that had slipped its branches through the window, strangled the victim in his sleep, then quietly closed the window again after. Another arboreal murder.

So okay, maybe everything you jot down isn't worth preserving. But for every killer tree, you'll find a dozen ideas that *are* still good, even in the cold, hard light of day, ideas that only need a little more nurturing to come into their own.

RULE 19.
Get Right,
or Get Close.

If you're writing an article about world-trade regulations, it's essential you get all your facts and all your statistics exactly right.

If you're writing a profile of a movie star or politician, it's critical that you record your quotes accurately.

If you're writing a history of warfare at sea, it's important that you know everything possible about clipper ships and aircraft carriers, sextants and sonar, torpedoes and Trafalgar, etc.

But—and this is a big but—if you're writing an imaginative work, something clearly billed as fictional, your responsibilities are a bit different, both to the reader and yourself.

First of all, you don't have to make yourself quite as crazy when it comes to the research. Oh, sure, if you want to make sure every single thing is scrupulously accurate and well documented, go right ahead. You can easily devote months, even years, to doing all the necessary research, to combing through library stacks, dusty archives, and baffling Web sites. You can prepare the factual ground for your work of fiction for as long as you like … but there's a good chance (I've seen it happen) that by the time you near the end of your research, you will also have lost the impulse that made you embark on it in the first place. You'll have gone beyond what was really necessary and lost yourself in the morass of detail.

In creating a work of fiction, you're asking the reader (or viewer, if it's a screenplay) to accept your take on the world—the world, that is, you've specially constructed for the purposes of your story. If you've done your job right, your audience is convinced of that world's plausibility and they're willing to go along for the ride. You don't want to do anything that will jar them out of that world—introducing, say, a Buick in ancient Rome or having a character speak in a manner clearly at odds with the tale: "Ride on, sir knight, we never meant to dis you."

But that doesn't mean you have to have cold, hard facts to back up every single thing in your narrative. In other words, if you're writing a story about Amsterdam, you can make up a canal or two. If you're writing a story about the CIA, you can imagine yourself, and your reader, into the inner sanctum. (The chances of your getting an invitation there are small.) If you're writing a sci-fi epic, you may even have to alter, or make up, some of the rules of travel in the space-time continuum. In one novel I wrote, I included some complex brain physiology, and I did hear from an old friend who'd become a brain surgeon. "You might want to give me a call," he advised, "the next time you're describing a brain dissection." Apparently, I'd placed a pesky little gland or two in the wrong spot.

Although he was undoubtedly correct, my other readers were never bothered. And so long as none of them trusted my novel to tell them how to do surgery, I was unperturbed. I felt I had done my job if I'd been able to carry them through that part of the story with enough verisimilitude that they didn't doubt my credibility or lose confidence in the world I had drawn them into. In fiction, veracity is nice—more power to you—but believability is all that you're really required to provide and all that your audience really has a right to expect.

In a close corollary to the rule above, there's one other thing to consider when creating your fictional world: How ordinary and familiar would that world be to a general audience? Because it makes a big difference.

I could get away with making a mistake in describing brain surgery (almost), but if I tried to describe a visit to the supermarket, where I spotted several movie stars loading their own carts, I'd be pushing my luck. Readers have shopped at supermarkets themselves—they know you seldom see celebrities there, and they know it's a pretty mundane experience all in all. Unless I can somehow account for those celebs (I'm shopping in Beverly Hills? There's a citywide strike of household staff?), I've violated reality to such an extent that nothing else I write is going to seem credible. I have ventured, whether I planned to or not, into the surreal.

A student once submitted to me a romance novel about a secretary who worked in Manhattan. She drove a Porsche, spoke several languages, and parked her car in the company lot before taking it out again to drive to lunch. I could get past the trilingual secretary with the

Know the Territory.

high-end sports car, but I somehow couldn't get past the company parking lot in the middle of Manhattan or the driving to lunch. I lived in New York, and I knew that that just wasn't the way life is lived there. People—secretaries especially—took the subway to work, and for lunch they walked around the corner to the deli.

The sheer pileup of unlikely details finally did me in, and I couldn't accept much else that followed in the book.

The better the locale is known (and New York, for instance, *is* known, through TV and books and movies, pretty much to everyone), the closer you have to adhere to its actuality. The same probably goes when you're writing about a few other spots— Chicago better not have palm trees, San Francisco better not be flat, Miami shouldn't be arid. If you're not familiar with these places and don't want to check your details, make up a town of your own, or place the action in a town less well recognized.

Follow the same precept when it comes to what happens. The more an experience is familiar to people—shopping at the supermarket, going to the dentist, washing the car—the more you have to stay true to it. Everyone knows how those go, and to alter them too much—unless you're doing it deliberately, for a reason—is to risk inducing in your readers an unwelcome crisis of faith.

RULE 21.

set

All writing is set somewhere.

In most nonfiction, the setting is determined for you.
If you're writing a magazine profile of a reclusive heiress, you
are going to need to describe the ten-foot hedge that conceals
her unmarked estate, the long winding drive that leads to the
ivy-covered Tudor manse, the bibelot-cluttered rooms. And
you would be crazy *not* to linger on these things. They not only
tell us about *how* she lives, they also tell us *who* she is. Setting,
in this respect, *is* character.

In fiction, you even get to choose the setting. (How lucky
can you get?) Your characters are going to live exactly where you
tell them to live. In rural Georgia? So be it. On the Gold Coast
of Chicago? Okay. Your choice of locale is, of course, going
to determine a great deal of what is to follow—it's going to be
hard to write a convincing rodeo scene set in New Haven—but
it's also going to color in your characters. If your hero lives in
Beverly Hills, then we might jump to the conclusion that he's
rich and privileged. But maybe he's not. Maybe he's living
there on a shoestring, in a run-down garden apartment, among
people he despises for the affluence and ease of their own lives.

Yourself Down.

That's why it's so critical that you address your setting in two ways: first, as you and your readers might perceive it, and second, as your character does. If he's living in the suburbs, is it by choice or because it's where his wife and kids wanted to go? It doesn't matter which you choose; what matters is that we feel the character is grounded, that he truly exists in a time and a place, and that we know how he feels about it. By positioning your character in a specific spot, you get to show him to us in either agreement with, or opposition to, the place. If, for instance, he feels marooned in the suburbs, he can rail about the boring barbecues and the identical green lawns. If he loves it, he can sing the praises of outdoor cooking and meticulous landscaping.

As an added benefit, the place, too, begins to assume character and dimension so that every time your hero sets foot on the train platform or the freshly mown grass, we not only know what he's thinking, we feel the impact of the surroundings ourselves. Bucolic, suburban paradise, or sterile, green hell—it could go either way, but either way it's going to add a lot to the picture.

Of the thousand and
one reasons not to write—and trust me,
I know 'em all—the one that lies at the base of most of them
is fear. Fear of failure, fear of success (I've heard of this one,
but I'm still not sure I believe it), fear of confronting whatever
personal demons and issues your writing may elect to address.
Do you tell it like it is, or do you sugarcoat the truth? Do you
keep your aspirations small—letters to the editor, fillers for the
local paper, jokes for *Playboy*—or do you kick out the jams and
take on an epic novel? Do you stop complaining about trying
to work at the kitchen table, surrounded by family commotion,
and take the bold step of renting a small office somewhere?

For all its rewards, spiritual and otherwise, writing is a scary
business. I wouldn't lie to you. You're facing more than the
blank page every time you sit down to work: You're facing a
silent challenge, even a reproach. *Go ahead*, that damn page says,
*give me your best shot—throw some words at me and let me show you just what
I think of them! I've faced down bigger opponents than you, and I ain't scared.*

**Whether you like it or not, you have now entered
what is commonly called a no-win situation.**

If you give in to your fears and let the blank page remain
unsullied, you will have simply traded one negative feeling—
fear—for another—regret. You'll not only feel bad about yourself, for cowardice in the face of composition, but you'll always
wonder what you might have been able to accomplish if you'd

RULE 22

Poison.

just forced yourself to blunder on ahead. Every time you go into a bookstore, you'll be looking at the new titles with a hint of envy in your eye, wondering how your own book might have stacked up to all these others and what it might have looked like—would it, too, have had a glossy cover, or something more discreet and tasteful? Even worse, one day you'll find on the shelf some book that reminds you of the one you were planning to write and it just won't be as good as yours would have been. That's a real killer. You'll want to yell at the top of your lungs, "Hold on! I had this idea! I can show you how this sort of book is really supposed to have been written!"

But of course you won't (not least of all because the security guard would throw you out of Barnes & Noble) but because it's too late—you had your chance and you didn't take it. That taste of ashes in your mouth is regret, and it's something even Listerine can't get rid of. But fear, on the other hand, why that evaporates with every word you write. Just do your work, and—mirabile dictu!—the fear will dissipate altogether and the regret, of course, never materializes. With any luck, the only thing you'll have left to contend with at the end of the day is your fear of success. (Write and tell me what that's all about.)

RULE 23. Bring Out da Noise.

Sometimes, the one thing keeping you from writing is the noise.

No, I don't mean the thumping bass of a neighbor's stereo,
the sirens from the street, or the lawn mower next door.

I mean the noise that's inside your own head.

There are voices in there, and they're not necessarily your friends.
They're harsh and critical and controlling. They say things like,
"That idea isn't so original," or, "Is that the best you can do?,"
or, "What makes you think you're a writer? You're an accountant,
for goodness sake!" It's like carrying around your own internal
Greek chorus of naysayers … and they never shut up.

But you've got to make them.

Nobody writes without her critical apparatus up and func-
tioning. You do need that voice that occasionally whispers in
your ear, "Let's find a better word for that," or, "Wouldn't
it be nice to insert an authoritative quote right here?" It's
called *thinking*. But you can't let that voice overwhelm you, slow
you down or, as can happen, bring you to a grinding halt.

Of *course*, there are things that are going to need fixing,
tweaking, rewriting. But that's what revisions are for. Right now,
if you hit a snag and you can't seem to get through it, just go
around. I will sometimes type, in all caps, gibberish where I know

something, or some section, needs to be gone back to. Or I'll throw in the initials TK, which stand, improbably enough, in journalism circles, for "To Come." I might need to know that I'm going to have to do some more research before filling in some portion of an article, but with a deadline looming (deadlines always help in this respect), I'll just skip ahead to a place where I *do* know the terrain and start writing there. (Although I don't *like* doing things that way—I like having all my ducks in a row before I begin—there are times when I don't have the luxury of that option.)

It's the perfectionist voice that does the most damage, the one that keeps kvetching about everything you do, that keeps telling you your stuff isn't good enough, that you should start over, that you shouldn't write the third sentence until the first two are pristine. Until you can quiet down that voice, and make a temporary truce with it, you will never get anywhere. You've got to make peace with yourself, some sort of pact that says, "You know what? I'm going to write as well as I can, and that's all I can do. And then, once I've got something down, I'm going to go back and see if I can make it better." If you have to, promise the perfectionist within that you'll never send anything out without giving it a thorough once-over, that you'll pay for a copyeditor out of your own pocket, that you'll tithe 10 percent of your writing income to a fund for dangling participles. Make any deal you have to … but shut down that voice in your head long enough so you can hear yourself think.

RULE 24

Map That Route.

Of all the words that bring dread to the heart of a writer, perhaps none does the trick better than "outline." Even typing it now makes my heart clench in my chest, my eyes glaze over, my thoughts flee. For me, the very word conjures up images of my eighth-grade classroom, with Mrs. Hughes standing at the blackboard explaining that for every I there must be a II, for every (a) there must be a (b), and so on. Whenever outlining is called for, I feel an irresistible impulse to run for my life.

And yet, I have seen the best minds of my generation tear out their hair and give up on some of their most promising efforts, all for want of an outline. I have seen friends rip into a screenplay, only to collapse in confusion in the middle of the second act. I have seen novelists stumble to a halt midway through their tale, the various threads of their narrative hanging between their fingers like tangled strings of Christmas-tree lights. I have read drafts of articles that circled back on themselves, that sprawled listlessly over page after page, and that had to stop, periodically, to remind the reader (and the writer) what the piece was about and what point it was trying to make. And though some of these mistakes would have emerged anyway—no one's first draft comes out perfect—outlining would have allowed the writer to avoid many of them.

But what do we mean by an outline? First let's get that straight. It doesn't have to be anything as formal as what Mrs. Hughes made us do. But it does have to be a plan—a serviceable road map that lays out most of the terrain ahead, the big scenes, the boffo conclusion. Obviously, an outline for a book or a movie script will have to be longer and more complete than one you would do for an article, but whatever the project, it will help you inestimably to have spent time, before you start writing, just sitting in a chair scrawling down all the things you plan to include in the piece. Some people use index cards, some have the luxury of corkboards or blackboards where they work. Some do what's called a "cluster" outline, simply by writing down the topic— "Halloween in the Heartland," say—in the center of a page, then writing all around it the various things the topic suggests. "Trick or treat," "popcorn balls and candy corn," "costumes," "pumpkin carving," "bonfires." Then, it's just a matter of connecting these parts to each other and mustering them into some sort of order with squiggly lines and arrows.

Plan your journey any way you want, with elaborate schematics, weird diagrams, or cryptic notes that even da Vinci could not crack, but do plan it. (If you want to make Mrs. Hughes happy, you can even do it the formal, old-fashioned way.) For every half-hour spent planning, you'll save countless hours, maybe even days, later on. And don't twist yourself into knots over it. Remember, you're not creating the fully fleshed-out body of the piece, you're just trying to create a rickety skeleton that will stand up long enough for you to hang the clothes on it later.

RULE 25.

And now, now that I've convinced you to make your plan,
be prepared to scuttle it.

The outline hasn't been written that a writer ever stuck to—
not all the way, at least. The outline, or whatever other plan you
might have drawn up, is one way you could have completed your
assignment; it's one way that would have allowed you to cover
all your material, or tell your whole story, from start to finish,
without too many detours or digressions.

But it was never the only way.

The beauty of writing, of any creative endeavor for that
matter, is in the discovery, and that part comes chiefly with the
doing of it. It's only as you write that your thoughts completely
coalesce, that your argument takes on its most persuasive form,
that your characters come alive, that your story suddenly swerves
in unexpected directions. It's only in the writing, I find, that you
fully wake up.

But that doesn't make your plan or outline any less useful—
your plan simply becomes, shall we say, malleable. Alter it all
you like, as weather conditions change. Make it conform to what
you're writing, and use it to look ahead and see what possible
problems might now have been created down the line. Did you

Wing It.

just give away a plot point that must, for other reasons, remain a mystery? Did you just kill off a character you're going to need later on? Have you stumbled onto a subplot, one that had never occurred to you when writing the outline, but that you now find neatly resonates with your main story? (That's a great feeling, when it happens.)

If it's nonfiction, ask yourself if you've established all the things you need to, and in the order they had to come. Say you're writing about physicists' latest plaything, superstring theory (better you than me, pal). Have you sketched in enough of the Newtonian, then Einsteinian, then quantum theory, to make your argument for seven dimensions immediately clear to even a lay reader? (Personally, I have enough trouble navigating in just three.)

Your outline is a crutch, there when you need it, and a solace when, in the dead of night, you think you'll never be able to figure out how to finish this project. The outline tells you it can be done, that, if all else fails, there's a working plan you can fall back on. But when you find yourself running ahead of it, when you see things unfolding naturally, organically, spontaneously before you, forget about the itinerary. Don't let any outline, plan, or diagram slow you up for even a minute. Just keep on running, and only take a break when you run out of breath, inspiration, or paper.

RULE 26.
Don't Look Back.

As my mother used to say, "A job worth doing isn't necessarily a job worth doing well."

This went for making beds, ironing pajamas, sweeping the back porch. It was enough, in her view, that it was done at all—it was pointless to put more time into it than the job warranted.

The same holds true, in my book, for first drafts. Because that's what they are—first drafts. Amateur writers hate to hear about drafts because they believe, truth be told, that once they've written something, it's done. They can hardly wait for the page to come out of the printer so they can get it into the mail and off to the publisher.

But real writers—writers who get published—know better. They know that a first draft is going to be a *working* draft, a first run-through for the finished product, full of accidental tangents and infelicities of style. But that doesn't stop them from turning one out—and, more importantly, it doesn't stop them from getting all the way from the start to the finish, from "Once upon a time" to "and they lived happily ever after."

That sounds easier than it is, and one reason many writers never get to the finish line of their first draft is because they keep looking back; they keep trying to fix every little thing on page ten before they move on to page eleven. For most of us, that is a formula for disaster—and incompletion. You will never get every word exactly right (I still cringe at certain passages when I read my old books). But if you plow ahead, if you make sure that every day you move your book or article or script just a *little bit* forward, eventually you will get to the end. Eventually, you will have a complete—however sloppy and prolix—manuscript. And that's when the real work begins: cutting, shaping, smoothing, and emending. In some cases, you will even want to go back and make wholesale changes, bolstering one character, eliminating another, dropping an entire section that no longer feels as essential as it once did. (Does your think piece about Britney Spears really need that long digression about the twelve-tone scale?) Whatever. But the only way to get to this polishing stage—to the second, or third, or fourth draft—is by completing the all-important first draft. And the only way to complete that first draft is to damn the torpedoes and go full speed ahead. Don't worry about the imperfect prose you may have left behind in your wake; you can, and you will, circle back again later and clean things up.

RULE 27.
Let It Marinate.

If there's anything better
than the feeling of satisfaction you
get from completing a piece of work, it's the
thrill you get from slapping it into an envelope and
mailing it off into the world. For days, weeks, even months
thereafter, you can go to bed at night dreaming of the call
you'll get from an editor or agent the next day, the deals you
will be offered, the extravagant sums that will be bandied about.
(Is it too soon, you wonder, to start looking into a numbered
Swiss bank account?)

But delightful as these fantasies are (and some may, indeed,
come true), the one thing that might stand in your way is
impatience.

**You may, out of an understandable eagerness to
see your work in print, let it go out the door before
it is really ready.**

You've prepared for this race a long time, so it's absolutely
critical that you do not jump the gun now.

No matter how long you've worked on the project, no matter
how many drafts you've gone through, it's a very good idea to
wait—just a little—before actually submitting it anywhere.

With an article or essay, it means holding on to it for a day or two. With a longer work, it might mean a couple of weeks. And that means not working on it, not even *reading* it, during that time. It *especially* means not reading it. Just let the work marinate, as it were, in your desk drawer or your computer file, and then, after enough time has passed that you can read it over with a passably fresh eye, do so.

You'll be amazed at what you find there.

Sentences that bump strangely, paragraphs that don't belong, bons mots that no longer seem so bon, typos, and misspellings. You'll wonder how you could have missed these things, but the answer to that one is easy: You were too close to the work. You knew every nuance of the prose, every beat, every twist and turn and transition. It's not that you couldn't see the forest for the trees—you couldn't see the trees for the twigs. What you needed was some distance, some perspective, and, most of all, you needed to get the rhythms of your own work sufficiently out of your head so you could encounter the work as strangers would, as your audience will. They don't *know* what's coming; they don't *know* where you're going. And now, when you read it over, ask yourself if you do. Are there spots where even you, the author, had to pause for a moment to get your bearings? Are there passages that weren't immediately clear even to you? It happens to every writer out there. But the good ones know that by holding on to the work for just that little extra bit, by giving it a final once-over in the cold light of a new day, they stand a much better chance of eventually seeing the work in print, or between covers.

Of course, for every writer who sends his work out into the world too soon, there's another who hangs on to it too long. My wife's a writer—and let me say that I love her dearly—but getting her to part with her work is harder than getting Pharaoh to release the Israelites. Until her editors call, cajole, and finally threaten legal action, she will not let the manuscript out of her hands.

Why is this? Why do writers hate to let go? Oh, I can think of several reasons, ranging from perfectionism to fear of rejection, but eventually, there comes a time when the work has just got to leave the premises. You've done your best, you've let it marinate, you've made any and all final corrections—it's time now to take it out of the drawer and put it into the reasonably capable hands of the postal service. The rest is up to fate.

Not sending the work out within an acceptable time frame is self-destructive in many ways.

If what you've been writing is an article, or even an essay, there's a good chance that something in it is timely, that the idea occurred to you because of something in the news, something you recently read, something you've noticed around you. Well, believe it or not, other writers out there may have taken notice, too. I can't tell you the number of times students in my classes have shown me work they thought was absolutely original and startling, only to discover that someone else, in the very same class, had already written on the same topic. There is a zeitgeist, a spirit of the age that surrounds all of us, all the time, and we all tap into it for our ideas. In Hollywood, it's common knowledge that, unbeknownst to each other, several screenwriters are simultaneously working on scripts based on almost identical premises. It happens all the time. Ideas are wafting in the air all around us, and working writers never leave home without their butterfly nets.

Delay can be fatal, too, because the longer the manuscript sits on your desk, unread, unsubmitted, unchallenged, the more stale and uninspired it will begin to appear in your own eyes, too. It's like something you once loved—that spiffy new overcoat, that painting you acquired to mount above the fireplace, your new boyfriend—which, with time, has lost its luster and allure. You stop noticing it, you stop holding it in such high regard—you start wondering, in fact, what you ever saw in it in the first place. You may be tempted to start tinkering, a process that, once begun, seldom ends happily. It's an all too common impulse, but before you give in to it, drop the manuscript in the mailbox, where you can't get at it again without committing a federal offense.

The thing about creating a fictional world is, sometimes it just stops turning. The action grinds to a halt, the characters stop talking to each other, nothing happens next. You sit back and no matter how long you stare at the screen or the legal pad, nothing seems to break the stalemate.

At times like that, it might pay to sprinkle a little movie dust on your own eyelids. Here's how: Lean back in your chair, close your eyes, and pretend that the story or novel or script you're working on (this works especially well for scripts) is up there on the screen and you're just a passive audience member, munching your popcorn and watching it. Roll back the action a few minutes, watch as the characters go through their paces and the action unfolds, and then, when it gets to the part where you're stuck, just try to keep the movie running. Let the scene go wherever it wants to, or let it change altogether if that's what happens. Try not to interfere. Let it surprise you. Does somebody suddenly jump out a window? Do a couple of the characters get into a shouting match? Does the scene abruptly halt, only to be followed by a drastically different one—a wild party followed by a hushed conference in a library? A tender love scene that turns into a jealous fight? An epic battle that gives way to a sorrowful morning after?

Call "Action!"
Pile It O

By letting your mind run free, and the movie in your mind unspool, you're not only trying out different alternatives—various ways the story can now move forward—but you're also, I believe, responding to something that has gotten you stuck in the first place. You weren't sure where to go next because you sensed your story needed a change—of pace, of tone, of setting. Something to shake it up and give it a jolt of whatever it had been lacking in the previous pages. If those pages featured small quiet scenes, then maybe what it needed now was something bigger, a scene at the circus or a bit of derring-do. If all it's been is derring-do, maybe it needed a passage with less suspense and more emotion. The movie in your mind is a good way of figuring that out. We're all so accustomed now to film techniques—pacing, cutting, split screens, slow motion, flashbacks, flash forwards—that turning your story into a mental movie is a lot easier than you'd think.

We are all budding Spielbergs! And putting yourself in the seat of a moviegoer—rather than an author—gives you a chance to imagine, freely, filmically, what your story truly needs to do the best at the box office.

When it comes to writing, there is perhaps no more vilified part of the language than adverbs. Even Stephen King in his book *On Writing* declares, "The adverb is not your friend." (I almost wrote that he *flatly* declares it, but that would be using one of the adverbs he so detests.) Like many writers, he considers them weak and weaselly, words that cling to other words—verbs, adjectives, and even other adverbs—draining them of impact or just cluttering up the page.

To King,

an adverb is a "pernicious dandelion,"

to be rooted out the first chance you get.

Whew—I get it already.

But I'm still not ready to concede the point entirely.

While adjectives modify nouns and pronouns—(a *pretty* girl, a *wounded* soldier, a *noble* stallion) adverbs give us the chance to modify verbs, usually with one of those words that end in "ly" (a pretty girl walked *confidently* into the party, a wounded soldier ran *wildly*, a noble stallion rose up *defiantly*).

What drives most opponents of the adverb up the wall is the fact that these adverbs are being used—in their heated opinion—

to do the work that a properly chosen verb, for instance, could and should have done on its own. For instance, instead of saying the soldier ran wildly, why not just say he charged? Instead of saying the stallion rose up defiantly, why not say it reared up? Isn't that easier and more to the point? Well, yes and no. In a lot of cases, it's true that the right verb can do the work on its own—and I, too, beseech you to search for the right one—but sometimes it can't. And I would submit that adverbs offer a lot of leeway and variety we wouldn't otherwise have.

Take that stallion rearing up, for example—couldn't he have reared up anxiously, out of fear? And wouldn't that have been misunderstood, if the "defiantly" had not been thrown in for additional clarification? In the hands of a better writer, maybe it would have been entirely clear why the horse was rearing up—maybe we would know from the previous pages that this was one brave, unruly stallion. But then again, maybe not.

Adverbs get used in many instances, like the one above, for emphasis. The writer isn't sure he's made his case clearly enough, so he throws in what amounts to another stage direction, just to assure himself that his reader is getting the right picture. Maybe it makes the writer look overly eager to please, like a suitor showing up at the door with flowers, chocolates, *and* a corsage, but you can't blame the poor guy for trying; he just wants to make the right impression, and there's something kind of endearing, if inept, about the attempt. If an adverb is the worst crime a writer commits, I'd say he's still worth dating.

RULE 31. Reduce Clutter.

While we're talking modifiers, I can't resist my favorite, which appears often in the Los Angeles real estate ads. Along with all the dubious, over-the-top tributes to the property for sale, some ads proclaim that this is "an *emotional* house." The first time I saw it, I thought it was a misprint. But it's not. While I can guess what the realtors, never known for their precision prose, are trying to say—that the house is so special it will *evoke* an emotional response in you—that's not what the ad as written is saying. Right now it's implying that the house has needs, feelings, and attitudes of its own, and I, for one, would not regard that as a selling point. What, you come home after a long day's work and *your house* is in a bad mood?

Adjectives, which should be one of a writer's best friends, can misfire. See above. They can be misused, attached so they suggest something not quite possible, or, more commonly, they can be scattered all over the page like confetti, where, instead of coloring the prose, they obliterate it. This adjectival overload, the most prevalent form of abuse, I lay at the door of creative-writing classes. Virtually every creative-writing teacher I had, from grade school through high school, encouraged drenching the story at hand in a thick syrup of goo. It was never a winter morning, it was always a "cold winter morning." It was never just a country inn, it was a "cozy country inn." No noun went into the world unmolested or unadorned.

And adjectives, like gang members, seldom ventured out alone. They went out in two and threes and, God help us, fours, and piled up on any person, place, or thing that got in their way. "Look! It's a noun—let's get it!" For the reader, it became a bruising experience as he tried to slog through the narrative without dropping from fatigue. When adjectives come, consistently, in pairs, or trios, or quartets—"The old red coach creaked down the long, winding, cobblestoned road and stopped before the timbered, mullioned, ancient tavern"—the hapless, weary, encumbered reader goes stark raving mad.

Adjectives are like spices you throw into the stew:

If they're helping, throw 'em in.

Judiciously. But the minute you sample the stew and it's the spices, not the stock, you're tasting, stop. You've gone too far

"What's wrong, Raoul?" she queried.
"Don't you love me anymore?"

"I'm not sure," he opined.

"Is it," she speculated, "someone else?"

"It's no one else," he expostulated. "It's this terrible scene we're trapped in."

Can't say as I blame him. But apart from the clichéd dialogue, what really makes the scene awful is all those ways the author (okay, that would be me) has found to avoid saying "said." And though I should no longer be surprised at this, I still come across writing manuals and instruction books, and even writing teachers, who encourage this kind of "creativity." (One mail-away course, I kid you not, included the example, " 'I might jump,' he vacillated as he edged towards the cliff." And this was *recommended*!)

In case no one has mentioned it before, I'm going to mention it now. The word "said" is an honorable one. It is, in every case, serviceable, and in almost every case, it is still the wisest choice for dialogue attribution. One of its greatest strengths is in its very ordinariness: No matter how many times you use it, it seldom, if ever, creates an annoying verbal echo in the reader's head. In fact, it hardly even makes a sound there. Your readers

It Again, Sam.

don't hear it any more than they hear punctuation. It's just a silent signpost, making sure they're able to keep the flow of the dialogue straight, so they can attend to the more important things, like what your characters are saying to each other and what, below the surface, they might really mean. And that, of course, is where you want their attention anyway.

Every time you search for a more interesting word than "said," and there are plenty of them out there, you run the risk of diverting the reader's attention, even momentarily, and of diminishing the efficacy and speed of the dialogue exchange. Sure, you can say, "she pleaded," "he demanded," and both of those verbs might add to the power of the scene—but they also might not. In almost every instance, "said" would have served, and if the scene is built well, so that we know who the characters are and what the discussion is about, we'll be able to gather the tone of voice just from the context.

Try this. The next time you're telling a story about what happened to you at work, or in class today, listen to hear how may times you say that someone declared, declaimed, admitted, confessed, announced, asserted, stated, or exclaimed, as opposed to the number of times you simply say "he said" or "she said." If it's good enough when you're speaking, it should also be good enough when you're writing.

RULE 33.
Show What You Know.

No matter how mundane you think your job is, to someone else it's interesting.

No matter where you grew up, even the most undistinguished of middle-American suburbs, to someone else it's unusual.

No matter how ordinary you think your family is, trust me on this one—to other people, it's bizarre.

It is all, as they say, in the telling.

The things you take for granted, the local landscape, the climate, the way people talk, the way they live their lives, is—or at least it can be—downright intriguing to people who lead their lives elsewhere, in other fashions. Did you grow up on the Great Plains in a town with two silos, a feed store, and a single diner? It might have been boring as bricks to the teenage you, but to someone who grew up on Park Avenue in New York, it might as well be Timbuktu.

Do you now work as a midlevel functionary in the municipal housing office? To you, it might seem the most colorless of occupations; to others, it might provide an interesting glimpse into the workings of city hall (*and* explain why their property taxes are as high as they are). Were you raised in a single-parent home, by your father, a fireman who moonlighted as an Amway salesman? (Wait—that one sounds like a sitcom in the making.) Any or all of these things—the substance of your life, the stuff you know in your very bones and fiber, the things you accept as so normal they are beneath real notice—all those things are as exotic as orchids to others, and, if written about with unruffled fidelity, they can be fascinating.

For Jane Austen, who led what many of us would think of as a circumscribed life, the slice of English society she observed and explored with such insight and acuity that her books have endured to this day, was all she needed. Barbara Pym, another of my favorite English authors, wrote about jumble sales at the vicarage and lonely spinsters in country towns, but again, she did it with such intelligence and sensitivity that her books can enthrall a guy like me, whose own life could not have been further removed from that milieu. We read those books for their truthful accounts of other worlds and eras, while we recognize in their stories, and their characters, the same emotions and human interplay we see in our own lives and relationships.

People read for two reasons: one, to go places they've never been before—Shangri-La and Paris in the spring, ancient Egypt and Persian palaces. And two, to go places they've been a million times but have never seen rendered into art, places they have never had revealed to them as acutely as you, the writer, have been able to do. Your pen can take your audience anywhere you please, but sometimes they'll be perfectly happy to just hang around the house with you.

RULE 34.
~~Get Dramatic.~~

But may I return, for one
moment, to Barbara Pym, whom
I just mentioned, the late author of a dozen or
so slim little novels set in mid-twentieth-century Britain?

Nobody in these books is a dashing English lord with a dark
secret. None is a ravishing beauty with an insatiable lust for
money and fame. There are no brutal murders, no ticking
bombs, no high political intrigue or perilous adventure. And
yet, these books can be as gripping as any page-turner churned
out by John Grisham or Patricia Cornwell.

What's her secret?

**In a word, it's her characters. And in another word,
it's the empathy she generates in us for them.**

Pym so expertly takes us into the lives of her heroines, into
their private desires and longings, their hopes and their fears,
that we begin to feel those dreams and defeats, those hesitations
and reservations, ourselves. We begin to root, ardently, for
these humble characters to get what they want, even if what they
want is for the vicar to accept their invitation to tea, or for their
contribution to the bake sale to be singled out for a prize. The
stakes are, by the standards of commercial fiction, never all that
important—the fate of nations never hangs in the balance, the

presidency is never threatened, the serial killer is not going to strike again—but the excitement runs high, nonetheless. It runs high because we have become invested in the people she has invented, and we want to see their modest hopes achieved, their unspoken longings addressed.

That, he said as if it were easy, is all you have to do. Create characters your readers care so deeply about that anything that happens to them *matters*. To do that you have to write about them honestly, clearly, with a kind of compassion (even for the bad guys). If you feel for them, there's a very good chance your readers will, too. And once that's done, the rest falls into place—we *care* whether or not they make the cheerleading squad, we *care* that they find their lost dog, we *care* about what's going to happen if they don't come up with the rent money.

The stuff of drama doesn't necessarily reside in Washington, D.C. intrigue or Beverly Hills luxe. Guns don't have to go off, bodies don't have to drop, the sex doesn't have to be hot and kinky (not that there's anything wrong with that); drama is generated when those characters we care about must struggle to get what they want. The more we empathize and identify with them, the more they live and breathe in our imaginations, the more we'll worry about them and turn the pages to find out what happens next. In the right hands, the saga of one young woman trying to find a place for herself in an indifferent city (see *Sister Carrie*) can be more enthralling than any international caper.

RULE 35

Heroes, by the way, don't have to be heroic.

In fact, the best protagonists, the ones that make a lasting impression, are decidedly not.

If you're writing about a central character who's virtuous, kind, strong, brave, handsome, well mannered, with good SATs, and a healthy respect for women, animals, trees, and cultural diversity, you are writing about a stiff, a guy too good to be true. And if he ain't true, he ain't believable, and if he ain't believable, why should we care what happens to him? *Nothing* can happen to him—he's a cartoon, and we all know that in cartoons, the characters can hold exploding bombs in their hands and emerge with nothing but smudged faces and spiky hair. They're indestructible, hence uninteresting.

A good hero or heroine is flawed. He has some failings, some things in his nature that aren't so admirable or likable. Maybe your character, though essentially good-hearted, was brought up in a benighted home, where brutality was a given; maybe some of that rubbed off. Maybe your heroine is willful and irresponsible, and her behavior winds up putting herself, and others, into some dangerous spots. Maybe she's generous, which

Flaw Your Hero.

initially makes us like
her, but so profligate with money that
that, too, winds up putting her family into a hopeless bind.
Maybe your hero is a man of action, but so quick and impulsive
in his judgments that his actions do more harm than good.

And maybe your protagonist has got some nasty habits.
John Self, the hero of Martin Amis's *Money*, is a drunk, a liar,
a chain-smoker, a philanderer, a slob, a spendthrift. But
because he is drawn with such humor and affection by the
author, we end up laughing with him and even hoping he
will get out of the many scrapes his bad habits get him into.

Mario Puzo's Godfather, Don Corleone, is not a good
man, either. He's a gangster, making his money off gambling,
prostitution, extortion, etc. But tell me you don't root for
him? Tell me you don't want things to go his way? One useful
trick Puzo employed, by the way, is worth mentioning. While he
admittedly made his hero—first the Don, then Michael his son—

bad guys, he made the other guys somehow worse. The kinky senator, the Sicilian drug dealer, the sadistic police captain, the pedophile producer. Most of the time, Puzo keeps your allegiances firmly on the wrong side of the law, but because of the expert way in which he has created his characters and manipulated the drama, you don't feel violated or betrayed.

Because your reader must see antiheroes like these completely in the round, in all their human frailty, they are the hardest to create and put over. We have to feel we really know them before we can move past their evil deeds, bad attitudes, and reprehensible conduct in order to ultimately forgive and even embrace them.

When creating your own hero, it's not a bad idea to keep the sandwich of the same name in mind—in other words, put in a lot of things, and add a few surprises. If he's all good—all fresh turkey and provolone—he's a snooze. You need to toss in some olives and anchovies, some red peppers and spice. Your hero has to be someone so winning as to hold our allegiance and interest but at the same time so imperfect as to be real.

By the same token, your bad guys can't be all bad, either. If they are, then they, too, become cartoons, malevolent machines whose actions and desires become predictable, linear, and, as a consequence, boring.

The monster in Mary Shelley's *Frankenstein* is a lumbering, lethal beast, but if that were all he was, the name of that book wouldn't even ring a bell today. Instead, Shelley created a character more sinned against than sinning, a creature we, as readers, know has no place on this earth, built as he is from the body parts of the dead, but for whom we feel sympathy and even sorrow. (And by the way, if you are relying on the Boris Karloff movies for your impression of the monster, then you are doing yourself a grave—pardon the pun—disservice: The book is still wonderfully readable, and the creature is far more complex, and even eloquent, than any movie version has given him credit for.)

If your antagonist is simplistic, monomaniacal, and flat, you're not giving your protagonist much to do, either. For your hero, it's the difference between playing tennis against a backboard and against a living, breathing opponent, someone capable of hitting the surprising drop shot or overhead lob back at him. A good villain brings out the best in your hero, forcing him to use all his own wiles and courage in order to gain the victory.

If you understand your antagonist, and you give him something more in the way of personality than a single broad streak of menace, then one problem you won't have is letting him come to life and speak his mind. For centuries, readers and critics alike have noted that the best lines in Milton's *Paradise Lost* go to Satan. The great villains—Simon Legree in *Uncle Tom's Cabin*, Inspector Javert in *Les Misérables*, Bill Sykes in *Oliver Twist*, Iago in *Othello*, Hannibal Lecter in *The Silence of the Lambs*—lend weight and power and meaning to the story; without them, in fact, there would be no story.

In fact, some of the top-notch villains are those who absolutely believe in their own rectitude; they don't think they're doing *bad*. They think they're doing *good*. And in response to such characters, the reader gets to experience all the emotions of anger, indignation, revulsion, and dread that are no fun in real life but great when it comes to a book or movie. He also gets to experience all the relief, even joy, at the end of the story when the forces of evil are defeated and the world is put right again. (Assuming, of course, that it is.)

As the writer, you get an added benefit: Villains are fun to write. There it is—I've said it. Milton knew it, Dickens knew it, Shakespeare knew it. With the hero, even a suitably flawed one, you still have to keep an eye on his likability, his values, and, especially these days, his political correctness. (Just firing up a cigarette in a no-smoking zone can cast him in a dim light.) But with the antagonists, you have none of those worries—villains can smoke, drink, lie, carouse, not to mention steal, pillage, swindle, commit murder. Not only that, they're encouraged to be bad. A villain whose worst crime is stealing hubcaps is not going to work up much emotion in your readers—or, for that matter, in you. If your characters—good or bad—don't inspire strong feelings, one way or the other, in you, their creator, there's not much chance they'll do it in folks who just stumble across them in the pages of your book or up there on a movie screen.

To write these bad guys, you are going to have to get in touch with your dark side—which, for many writers, isn't easy. We write to enlighten, to amuse, to entertain our audience, and the very notion of creating evil (even in imaginary form) can seem foreign or wrong. As a result, the antagonists can wind up as pushovers or cardboard cutouts. That's why it's especially important, when developing them, that you put in the same amount of effort and thought that you did in creating their virtuous counterparts. Give your villains a background, a backstory, and all the humanizing traits you can stand. We'll hate them all the more for it.

The truth, you've undoubtedly heard, can set you free.

Well, it can also tie you into knots.

If you're writing a biography, a serious scientific paper, or a company report, then by all means let the truth be your guide. (Or try to.)

But if you're writing an imaginative work—a novel, a story, a screenplay, even a memoir—the most dangerous thing you can do is worry too much about a silly old thing like the truth.

Many's the time I've been presented with a work in which something not quite credible or convincing appeared, and when I brought it to the writer's attention, he or she shot back, "But that's what really happened!" It's said in all earnestness, as if the truth were the best defense, and as if, just because the incident actually occurred, it had to be rendered exactly as it went down, no matter how undramatic, improbable, or fundamentally irrelevant that was. Whether you're writing a work of fiction or a nonfiction account of, say, a nightmarish family car trip, your first allegiance is not to the truth but to your audience. If all we wanted to read was a blow-by-blow account of that dreadful car trip, we'd ask for a complete transcript and a copy of the itinerary. But that's not what we want.

the Truth

Writing is an act of distillation, of separating the wheat from the chaff, and, most important of all, giving shape to the shapeless.

In life, one thing follows another, seldom with any apparent logic, and sometimes without any clear causation. In art, we have to impose that logic, we have to give the audience a sense that things happen for a reason and that they happen in a certain order for a reason. Is this lying? Sure—all art is a lie. But it's a lie told in the service of a greater truth. Even a photograph doesn't capture the truth—it captures what one photographer, armed with one camera, perceived and recorded in one split second. What did he get in the frame? How did he compose it? What did he leave out (that you'll never know)?

In the same way, every time you choose one word over another, you've subtly altered the truth and how your readers will understand it. Every time you rearrange the words you're using to describe an incident, you're changing the incident; you've messed with reality, with "what really happened." But far from feeling bad about it—or, even worse, beholden to the historical record—you should go right ahead and do it again. As an artist, *that's your job*—to take the raw material and sculpt it into something powerful and whole. Maybe something hard to believe really *did* happen—but that's no reason we should have to believe, or accept, it as is. Mold it for us into a plausible narrative event, and maybe then we'll go along for the ride. Maybe then we'll be able to get past the facts and see the truth.

RULE 38.

Strip Down to Your Briefs

If you've already heard this anecdote, forgive me.

But the eminent French philosopher Pascal once wrote a long letter to a friend, apologizing at the end for its length. He didn't have time, he explained, to make it shorter.

Ring any bells? There isn't a writer on the planet who hasn't written a few extra words now and then, who doesn't need to read over her work and do some judicious pruning. And when it comes to the heartfelt stuff, like letters and memoirs, the problem is only exacerbated. Who wants to stop midstream to start clearing up the clutter and editing the revelations pouring forth like water from a secret spring? Better to let it flow—we all know how hard it is come upon a gusher—and worry about the cleanup later.

But worry about the cleanup, we must. When you write something needlessly prolix and convoluted, there's a reason for it, and that reason is usually a lack of clarity and purpose going in. Something in you—an impulse to get some thoughts down on paper, an urge to vent or passionately communicate your feelings about something—took hold, so you started writing. So far, so good. There's gold in that rushing stream, but to find it you'll have to do some careful panning.

Only after you run out of breath and read over everything you've written will you really be able to see, and extract, the point and the pith of what you were saying. Writing long is easy because you're not really doing one of the hardest things about writing—which is editing—as you go. Writing long is a way of searching for the truth, or the argument, as you go along and asking the reader to accompany you on the ride. You may be able to make the trip so diverting, he doesn't mind. Or—and this is, sadly, more likely—you may leave him stranded by the side of the road, halfway to the intended destination, wondering what that was all about and where, if anywhere, he was supposed to be going. Writing long is a perfectly good way to explore every avenue of thought, every possible turn in the road, every available sight along the way.

There's a lot to be said for letting your typing fingers or scribbling pen outpace your conscious intellect, your inner censors, and even your better judgment.

But once that's been done, it's wise to retrace your steps, eraser in hand, and figure out what, after all, would have been the most direct route.

RULE 39. Go Subliminal

Of the many reasons to write, one of the strongest is the urge to send a message, to communicate some strongly held view you have and, by so doing, open the eyes of the world to a great injustice. (And maybe, just maybe, do something to correct it.) Harriet Beecher Stowe did it when she wrote *Uncle Tom's Cabin*. Upton Sinclair did it when he wrote *The Jungle*. John Steinbeck did it when he wrote *The Grapes of Wrath*. Rachel Carson did it when she wrote *Silent Spring*. Betty Friedan did it when she wrote *The Feminine Mystique*.

You might be next.

But when you're writing with a message in mind, you have to be careful. It's one thing if it's nonfiction—there you're entitled to write a polemic, full of sound and fury, statistics, examples, and complex arguments on behalf of your cause. The same for editorials, or their junior cousins, the ubiquitous letters to the editor. Make your case as boldly and convincingly as you can, using all your powers of persuasion and every trick you can pull out of your bottomless writing bag.

But if you're planning to convey your message in some other way—through, for instance, fiction—then you have to tread very carefully.

People who read an editorial are expecting one thing; people who pick up a novel **are expecting quite another.**

People who read an editorial are expecting to be confronted, lectured, even hectored; people who read fiction are expecting, no matter how serious the subject matter, on some level to be entertained. They're not planning to attend a debate, they're planning to enter another world, an imaginary world, created and populated by you, the author, and in which they hope to lose themselves for a few hours, even a few days. If they wanted to pick a fight, they'd go to the local bar; if they wanted to educate themselves about the inequities of global food distribution, they'd log on to the appropriate Web site or go to an open lecture at a nearby university.

The pact you make when you ask a reader to pick up your work of fiction is to deliver a *story*, an imaginative, cohesive (which doesn't mean it always has to be immediately coherent) tale.

If there's an underlying message—that we don't do enough for the homeless, that the war on drugs does more damage than the drugs do, that the minimum wage is too minimum—that's fine, but the message shouldn't be baldly stated. The reader shouldn't feel like he's been bludgeoned over the head or even panhandled on the street. He should simply leave the world of your fiction with a greater insight into the subject you were writing about, and perhaps a greater fellow feeling for the people buffeted by the adverse forces you've described. Your readers should be first-class passengers on the train of your narrative; they should be traveling comfortably, unaware of the heavy freight that's being transported, unseen, right along with them.

RULE 40.

Not long ago I went to a public event sponsored by a local university where unpublished, or struggling, writers could read aloud from their works in progress. And while I did not expect to be bowled over by the offerings, I did come away shocked— shocked by how uniformly *good* the selections were. The prose I heard that night was carefully wrought and often beautifully expressive, and though I had planned to stay only half an hour or so, I wound up sitting there, on that hard fold-up chair, for the full evening.

But I did start to miss one thing. In all these skillfully rendered selections, there was little, if any, sense of movement, of change. Everything was extraordinarily well observed and described, but that alone seemed to be the point of the writing—to capture a scene, a moment, a fleeting mood. The pieces I heard that night seemed, by and large, to be in stasis, or something darn close to it. If there was any conflict, it was in a distinctly lower key; if there was any change in a character's situation, it was so modest as to be almost imperceptible. If anything actually happened, it was off-screen, downplayed, or barely acknowledged.

Now, not everything we read needs to be plot-driven; not everything needs to be Tom Clancy or Michael Crichton or Mary Higgins Clark. But I must admit that when I hear the work of authors like these disparaged, I want to spring, quite unnecessarily, to their defense.

Cook Up a Story.

Building a story that keeps readers turning the pages, **creating a narrative structure with a sense of momentum,** where one event leads to another and the final outcome remains in doubt, **is a remarkable feat—** and the reason these writers get paid such princely sums to keep doing it.

(Sometimes the ending is where we start, and the rest of the story is essentially a flashback—read *Double Indemnity*, see *Sunset Boulevard*—but the fun there is in seeing what happened to reach that climax or conclusion.)

With all the attention to fine writing these days, and the myriad creative-writing programs in high school, college, and beyond, it's easy to focus on the art of writing, on nuances of language and the graceful evocation of mood. But at the same time it's critical that you keep that sturdy old workhorse of story firmly in your sights. If your story doesn't *have* much of a story, it's likely to remain inert. All those characters you've so lovingly created have nothing to do. All your clever dialogue in the end has little to convey. All your well-crafted scenes don't accrete or lead on to one another—they simply exist like sparkling gemstones that have never found a common setting. But find a solid story and you will bring them all together into one truly fabulous piece of jewelry.

Rumor has it
that a writer died and
left instructions that on his
tombstone should be inscribed,
"At last, a plot!" Which just goes to show
you how tough it is to come up with one.

Lord knows I've beaten my own head against the wall for
countless hours in search of good, fresh, ingenious plots.
And I've been told, as no doubt have you, that there are no
completely original ones left. There are, according to whichever
authority you listen to, three main plots, or six, or a dozen, and
everything else is just a minor variation on one of them. And
maybe it's true. What I do know is that every plot you come up
with will, at some point, start to remind you of some other plot
in a book you've read or a movie you've seen. Read enough,
see enough flicks, and before long you'll have such a wide frame
of reference that virtually everything you think of will bounce
off of, or call to mind, some story you're already familiar with.
Eventually, you may despair of ever finding anything new.

But maybe that's because you're overheating your dynamos.
Instead of trying to come up with some big idea—a ticking bomb
on the President's plane, a deadly plague, a cop who
can tap into the mind of serial killers—try thinking small.
Try thinking, specifically, of your characters, not your plot.
If you're not sure what the action of your story should be,
forget about it for a while and focus instead on the people

involved. No matter how strong a plot is—or how "high-concept," to use the Hollywood parlance—it won't amount to much, anyway, if the characters aren't engaging or memorable.

So, sit back and relax. Visualize your characters. Who are they? What do they look like? What are their hopes, their fears, their desires? And how will getting what they want somehow put them into conflict with others?

I've seen it recommended that you create a whole back story and bio for all your characters—where they went to school, how many siblings they had, what their favorite pet was, etc. If it works for you, try it. Personally, I've always been too lazy. But I do try to figure out what will set my characters into motion, how they will wind up colliding, and what will happen as a result of that collision.

If even that doesn't work, then I take a different tack. I think about introducing a new or different character; sometimes it just takes adding something to the mix—a mean boss, a flirtatious neighbor, an overbearing mother, or a long-lost brother—to kick the story into gear. And because the action evolves from the peculiar interactions of characters that only you could have brought to life and to the page, and not from some mechanical and superimposed plot, it'll all sound and feel original. Daunting though it may be, plot is really nothing more than credible characters bumping up against each other and, ideally, leaving some bruises, some kisses, and some complaints.

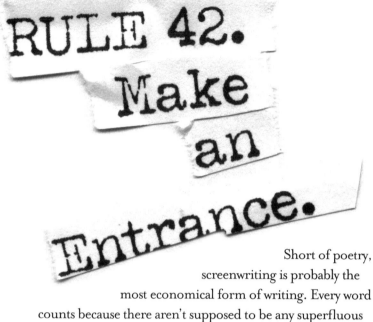

RULE 42.
Make an
Entrance.

Short of poetry,
screenwriting is probably the
most economical form of writing. Every word
counts because there aren't supposed to be any superfluous
words at all—the script is supposed to be as lean and clean as a
blueprint.

And it was from a veteran screenwriter that I learned one
of the paramount rules of his trade, when I was writing my first
TV script.

**"Always arrive late and leave early," he said,
and though at first I rejoiced, thinking he was
talking about the office hours, I soon learned that
he was referring to the script I was working on.**

It seemed, in retrospect, a good rule for pretty much any
kind of writing.

Figure out what the action of the scene is going to be, or what
its thrust is, and then start writing just a fraction before that
action begins. In other words, if the scene takes place in a lecture
hall, ask yourself if we really need to see the students filing in, the
professor clearing his throat, the lecture being given, before we

get to the crux of the matter, which is the argument that erupts between the professor and your protagonist, in which your protagonist is thrown out of school. If *that's* what the scene is about, if that's what moves the action of your story forward, then come in just before the argument flares up and out of control. And once the expulsion notice is given, end the scene— or "Cut!" as they say in the movie biz. Lingering in that lecture hall will only dilute the power of the confrontation.

Whatever you're writing, even if it's an article, an essay, or a letter, there's an irresistible tendency to meander. And that's understandable in the first draft. But when you're doing the revision, look again at that prologue material and see how much of it you really need. Most of the time, you'll find that it's simply holding your reader at arm's length and maybe, in the worst case, boring him to tears. It's like that guy at the office who takes so long to get to the point of his story that everyone's left the watercooler by the time he does.

The same goes for knowing when to quit. When the action of the scene is completed, when the point has been made or the punch line delivered, do not hang around. Anything else you say at this point can only weaken what came before. Quickly look for the nearest exit, and go through it.

As I am doing now.

RULE 43. Do Double Duty.

And while we're borrowing from the screenwriter's bible, here's another little nugget that often serves well for other kinds of composition.

When you're writing a scene, look at the action. Look at what happens in the scene. Do a couple of your characters get in their car and drive across town to have dinner? Okay, fine, but now ask yourself this: Is that all that happens in the scene? Do we manage to overhear the two discussing their respective days or, better yet, bickering about where to eat? We're getting there. But look harder at the scene, and ask yourself again—is all we're seeing a drive and a squabble?

If that's the case, then the scene is probably what we call, in the script business, shoe leather. That means it's a scene that accomplishes little more than, literally, getting some people from one place to another or laboriously establishing some necessary plot point. To be blunt, if all that's happening in your scene is what's happening in your scene, then it probably isn't earning its keep. (I believe this rule, by the way, originated with the eminent screenwriter William Goldman, though it was first passed along to me by a producer I once worked for.)

In other words, what you want to invest the scene with is some subtext,
an emotional or thematic burden
that gives the surface action some greater heft and purpose.

The surface action of the scene doesn't have to be anything special. In some ways, the more mundane it is, the better. Your characters can simply be playing cards (see the play *The Gin Game*), or motoring around town on errands (see *Driving Miss Daisy*), or discussing any ordinary, everyday matter at all (see almost anything written by Raymond Carver, Frederick Barthelme, Anne Beatty, or Richard Russo). It's while they're going about these routine things that they are simultaneously revealing important things about themselves, about each other, and about the way in which they view the world. It's not in the overt actions of the scene, or even in the dialogue per se; it's in the things that are left undone, the words left unsaid, the evasions and elisions, the hesitations and prevarications and unexpected gestures. In Paddy Chayefsky's *Marty*, Marty and his pals regularly ask each other, "What do you want to do?" It's the flattest, most desultory conversation imaginable, and yet the repeated plaint comes to painfully suggest the depths of the loneliness and aimlessness of the guys' lives. It's a poignant cri de coeur, disguised as an offhanded remark, and it's writing at its simplest and most sublime.

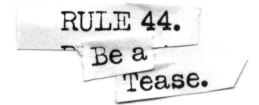

RULE 44.
Be a Tease.

In all writing, as in l'amour, it pays to be a coquette.

Whatever your message is, whatever you set out to convey to your reader, it's never a good idea to deliver too much, too soon. Your reader is not only unprepared, but he can be, quite frankly, disappointed.

If someone's reading your editorial, he wants to be persuaded. He wants to see your argument unfold, and your conclusion reached, as if inexorably, by the irrefutable train of logic you have presented. Even if ultimately he chooses to disagree, he wants to understand where you started and how you got there—if only to write his own scathing rebuttal the next day.

If it's fiction, then your reader needs time, and pages, to acclimate herself to your world and get her bearings. Throw too much at her too quickly—an exotic locale, a wide cast of characters, an abundance of action—and she may feel overwhelmed and unable to catch up. If this sensation lasts too long, she'll find some easier way to occupy those precious leisure hours. (If there's one thing that causes me to put down a novel after just five or ten pages, it's when I get that feeling I've stumbled into a huge family reunion where everyone else is right at home, catching up and swapping stories, and I know no one in sight.)

Suspense is a necessary component of any writing; without it, we'd never go from one sentence to the next. Even in a letter to a friend, you are creating some kind of narrative, a concatenation of events (I love that word, "concatenation"—just say it out loud and catch the rhythm) that will carry your friend along.

You're building a story, or an anecdote, or a scene from your recent vacation, bit by bit, and as you add each detail, the picture becomes more complete. But the art of that is as much in the withholding as it is in the telling.

Every time you choose what to write next, you are withholding something else; you are essentially putting things in order. First in your head, and then on the page. Whenever you hit a snag in your work—especially while writing nonfiction or journalism—you can often trace it back to something you said too soon, without having set it up properly or having put it in the proper context. As a result, other things have begun to pile up in an unseemly pile, and you soon find yourself trying, with increasing desperation, to straighten it all out. Unfortunately, the more you flail around, the worse things usually get. It's far better, in general, to go back and pinpoint where you jumped the gun. Then, you can crouch down in the starting block again and prepare to run that leg of the race all over.

In some ways, this—keeping
the faith—is the hardest of all the
problems any long-form writer faces.

If all you're writing is an editorial, a short
essay, even a brief article, you can do it in one or two sittings.
In fact, the best think pieces, to my mind, are the ones that
do spring from one session, as if exhaled in one long breath.
They usually have a clarity, a consistency of tone, a wholeness
that long-aborning pieces can't quite manage.

But a book or a screenplay requires a sustained effort, over
months, even years and, even worse, a delay in the ultimate
gratification—of publication or production. Your editorial may
appear in the paper the next day, but your book may take years
to appear on a shelf; your screenplay may take years to get produced and shown in theaters. And in the meantime, all
your friends will drive you mad with well-meaning questions
like, "So how's the book coming? When can I buy a copy?"
and, "Who's going to be starring in the movie? Will it be out in
time for Christmas?" (Truth be told, I don't think all those
queries are so innocent; some, I suspect, are slim as shivs, deftly
inserted where the pain will be the greatest.)

But such questions will have their effect, chiefly because they
echo the same questions ringing in your own head. When *will*
this thing ever be done? Is it worth all this trouble and energy?
What, exactly, was it supposed to be about? (And why doesn't it
seem to be about that anymore?)

You have come, to conjure Dante, to that "dark wood where the straight way is lost." You have lost your faith along with your bearings. And you wonder if you will ever get either one of them back again.

You will.

Your bearings will come back more easily. Merely taking that break, recommended earlier, will probably open your eyes to the technical problems, and to their solution.

Your faith, well, that's trickier, isn't it? It's a real conundrum. To get it back, you just have to believe—in yourself, your work, your mission. One thing that might help is knowing that virtually every other writer has encountered these same problems, has entertained these same doubts, has dropped his head onto the desk and wondered why it wouldn't be a better idea, after all, to take up clog dancing or bird spotting. (Could it be that all those amateur ornithologists and avid clog dancers are, in fact, blocked writers?) And some writers, it's true, have given up. I cannot tell a lie.

But most of them—like you, I hope—eventually remembered what drove them to do this in the first place, the impetus that set them on their way. The spark that started the fire is still glowing, and all it takes to bring it again into flame is a breath or two of air. And wouldn't it be a shame to let it die down now, what with all those pages, already written, sitting in the cardboard box under the desk?

All those pages that your friends secretly believe you never wrote?

If nothing else, don't you want to be able to wave a published book under their noses one day? Wouldn't that be sweet?

The baser instincts should never be underestimated as a spur to higher things.

As a national policy, conservation is good.

It's even good as part of your daily life.

But as a writing technique, it stinks.

I actually had a writing student who was full of colorful anecdotes and great story ideas but whose written work never quite measured up. Sometimes that's just due to a lack of writing ability, but that wasn't the case here.

The stories she'd turned in were perfectly well written; they just weren't about very much, and they were nothing like the rich trove of material she'd share with me in office conferences, or even out loud in class. When I finally asked her why she thought this was, she answered without a moment's pause, "Because I'm saving that stuff."

"Saving it? For what?"

"My novel."

I should have known.

Like many writers, she felt like she had to conserve her A material for the project that was always just around the bend. (She was already in her late twenties, so I don't think it would have been too hasty of her to spend a little of this literary capital.) The good stuff was too good to waste on class assignments and short stories; it was destined for greater things, for the glittering showcase of a novel.

And while I'm all for writing novels, I am not for the pickling of literary material. For one thing, you may think you're saving it up for later use, but in fact you're letting it get stale, you're letting it lose some of its vitality. Material you think is unforgettable today, you will have forgotten by this time next year.

Fortunately, by then you will have accumulated much more. Writers who fear using their best stuff are worried that there won't be any more where that came from. They're afraid that they're going to run out, when that, in fact, is the one thing you never have to worry about. As long as you're alive, you're accumulating new material all the time. Not to mention perspective, insight, understanding. (You'll note that I don't say you *behave* any better; I do say that you might have a better notion of why you *mis*behave—and that's something.)

Conventional wisdom has it that we get more conservative as we get older, but I think the opposite is often true. (It certainly is in my case.) As we age, we learn to accept things our parents may have taught us were unacceptable; we see things, even in our friends, that we have to learn to live with. We encounter adversity in even the most blessed lives. We get a wider, more experienced, all-encompassing view of life, and that view informs everything we write, adding scope and depth to the work.

Our best stuff gets even better, and the more we use of it, the more we seem to have.

RULE 47. Lay Down the Law.

Nobody likes a namby-pamby—and least of all in an author.
When you're writing, you're creating your own world on the page,
and in that world you are God. So act it.

Readers don't need to agree with you, they don't even need to like you, but they do need to feel that you are in control of that world; they need to know that even if it's only a wizard behind the curtain, there *is* a wizard.

A few years back, there was a brief vogue in publishing circles for "make your own adventure" books, books that contained alternate endings and left it up to the reader to choose among them. (I was even asked to write one of these.) Want a happy ending, where the lovers reunite? Choose Ending A. Want a more downbeat, perhaps realistic, conclusion? Choose Ending B, where they part at the bus station, wiser but wearier.

These books failed, and for the very reason that I knew enough to turn down the one that was offered to me. Readers don't *want* to have to choose their own ending, any more than they want to have to choose their own beginning or middle. If they could do all that, they'd write the books themselves, and they wouldn't need authors at all.

Writing is choosing—this word over that one, this twist instead of that turn. We read certain writers because we have come to trust and enjoy their choices—we know, when we read a tale by Dickens, that there's going to be a very large cast of characters,

bafflingly intertwined, and that in the end everything will be sorted out for us. By the same token,
when we read a lengthy article by one of our
favorite journalists, we trust the writer to
introduce us to his subject, guide us through
the intricacies of his argument, and conclude in
a memorable fashion. He's done it before, why
not again?

Open-endedness is fine, in small doses.
(Who among us was not assigned Frank R.
Stockton's "The Lady, or the Tiger?" in junior
high?) But when we sit down to read a whole
book, watch an entire movie, or plow through
a substantial piece, we want to feel that the hand
guiding us by the elbow is a firm one. Even the
most open-minded, experimentally tolerant
among us (and I'm not one) wants to know
that somebody else has given this material a lot
of thought, because if no one has, why should
we spend our own time trying to unravel it?

Art can be as challenging as you want to
make it—as challenging as you think your
audience can stand. But remember that,
ultimately, your readers are counting on
you to get them out of the forest again,
and the last thing they want to hear from
you is, "Geez, I don't know—where do *you*
think we are?"

RULE 48.
Keep Your Promises.

Your readers are counting on you for something else, too. They're counting on you to follow through on the promises you've made.

"What promises?" you may ask. "I barely know these people."

Well, that doesn't matter.

Any time you write something, and expect others to read it, you are making them a promise of one kind or another.

If it's a travel article, you're promising to give them a thorough portrait of the place you're describing and to leave them with sufficient information to decide whether or not they'd like to visit that place themselves.

If it's a think piece for the newspaper, you're promising to deliver a cogent argument, one that opens their minds to new possibilities.

If it's a movie script, you're promising to tell an involving story, one that has a beginning, a middle, and an end (preferably in that order), that ties up all the loose, untidy plot strands and leaves your audience feeling satisfied.

Not to mention the most fundamental promise of them all. Every time you pick up your pen, you are suggesting a deal: In return for the readers' time and attention, you are offering entertainment. It doesn't have to be crazy car chases or hot love scenes, but it does have to be interesting. It does have to take your readers somewhere they've never been, show them something they've never seen, teach them something they've never known. That's the implicit deal you've made, and your readers, even if it's never been spelled out, know it as well as you do.

When you finish a piece of work, and you've let it cool down like a pie on the windowsill, read it over and look for all the issues you've brought up, the expectations you've raised, the plot points you've made. How well have you delivered on them all? In your editorial, did you play fair, and at least allude to the opposing point of view, before concluding your definitive argument? In your travel piece, did you remember to mention that this island paradise has no potable water? In the screenplay, did you resolve all the major conflicts on which the story turned, or are your moviegoers going to stop on the way back to their cars and say, "Well, wait a minute—did they get the diamonds or not?"

> Don't break your promises. Keep them—
> and you'll keep your public coming back.

The worst editors I know are the ones who assign you a piece and then, when you ask them how long they want

the piece to be, say, "Oh, let's just see what it comes in at."

Mostly, this happens at magazines and newspapers, but it can be a problem with whatever you're working on. Why?

Because length matters. (No jokes, please.)

The length of a manuscript, whether it's a magazine feature or a novel, determines a whole host of other practical and aesthetic decisions you have to make along the way—and if, going in, you don't know what that length is supposed to be, you are laboring under a great handicap.

First and foremost, there is the question of pace. If you've been assigned, say, an article on how to buy a used car, you need to know how many words you're supposed to write because, without that number, you don't even know what kind of lead to write. If all you've got is 750 words, then you're going to start out with—and keep up—a very brisk pace; you're going to jump right into the piece, without preamble, and probably deliver your main points in a bullet style. But if, instead, you've got 2,500 words to squander, then you might decide to make your lead anecdotal—you might choose to introduce a lovely young couple, clutching their checkbook, timidly stepping onto the used-car lot and hoping to emerge with the car they'd been dreaming of. (Fat chance.)

Your style throughout the piece is going to differ, too, depending on the word count. Longer pieces allow, obviously, for a more effusive style (though they don't necessarily insist

Hit Your Marks.

upon it). Shorter pieces require a quick, get-to-the-point approach. Again, it helps to know the score ahead of time.

Length also determines how and when you deliver your important information. In the case of the used-car article, for instance, you'll be wanting to touch on floor-mat negotiations, rust proofing, factory rebates, etc. And if you're writing short, all this stuff will be compacted and up-front: bang, bang, bang, and you're out of there.

Writing long, these issues will be measured out, possibly in teaspoons. Every couple of hundred words, you should be taking on another major point or issue. And if you keep one eye on the finish line, you can always gauge the distance remaining and either pick up, or slow down, your pace accordingly.

But what about when you're writing for yourself—"on spec," as they say? Isn't it a great comfort and relief not to have to worry about length, to just sit down and let 'er rip? Well, sure, and that is one of the beauties of writing without an assignment in hand or an editor looking over your shoulder: The material dictates the length.

But in my experience, the material can also run amok. It can refuse all attempts to be reined in, governed, or even shaped. Without a clear idea of what you're writing (a slim memoir? a bulky family saga?), you don't know how to set your internal metronome. You don't know whether to set the pace at adagio or andante. Write a chapter, and once you're satisfied with it, study its rhythm. That's the rhythm you probably want for the rest of the book, and it in turn will help you to define the length and the scope of the project. Listen to the ticking.

RULE 50.

Don't Push Your Luck.

Okay, so you were once having lunch with a friend, complaining about your untrustworthy boyfriend, when, of all people, who should come in and sit down at the very next table? The cad himself—with a date.

"What a coincidence!" you might think (as you fumble for your steak knife).

And, if you were to use this situation as a kick-start for a story or a movie, it'd be perfectly okay. Coincidences do happen. That's why we have a word for them.

But they *don't* happen all that often. If they did, they wouldn't be coincidences anymore. They'd just be more of that random stuff that happens to us every day.

When Ilsa walks into Rick's bar in *Casablanca*, that's a coincidence—such a whopper, in fact, that the script even acknowledges it by having Rick mutter, "Of all the bars, in all the world, she has to walk into mine." (In movie parlance, by the way, that's called "hanging a lantern" on it—openly admitting to something that might otherwise strain the credulity of the audience and distance them from the story. By pointing at it yourself, you've acknowledged the audience's question, shared it with them, and as a result you can all put it behind you and move on from there.)

Audiences, and readers, will forgive you for using coincidence at the start of a story. It's sort of a given, a way that so many stories employ to set everything else into motion. If Ilsa hadn't walked into that bar, there'd *be* no *Casablanca*, and we would all have been the losers thereby. But, as the author, you have now spent your "coincidence capital." You've used your free pass, and another one is going to be awfully hard to come by.

If you really feel you have to—if your story provides you with no other way around it—and you just *have* to use another coincidence, then you should know that your audience is going to raise one very large and very skeptical eyebrow. They'll feel like you're cheating—and, in a way, you are.

With one caveat. If your extra coincidence makes things *worse* for your hero—if the office worker playing hooky at the track bumps into his boss at the betting window—that's somehow more acceptable than if, while playing hooky, the same guy stumbles across a bag full of money. Maybe it's just that people are more likely to believe that bad things can happen all the time, and maybe it's because the second bad coincidence has the salutary effect of making the story more difficult or dangerous for your hero. Whatever the reason, keep your coincidences to a minimum—and, if you must use them, lean toward the unlucky ones.

What would a book for writers be without a chapter on those two most infamous words of all: writer's block? Heck, I don't even like to type those words. Not because I'm scared of them, but because I don't like to give them any greater credence than they already have.

Nonfiction writers, to begin with, seldom suffer from writer's block—for a fairly simple reason. If you're writing a biography, you can always move on to the next big chapter in your subject's life; if it's a book on military hardware, you can move from tanks to rockets; if it's a monograph on Cézanne, you can address the next painting.

The path ahead—or at least one *possible* path— is generally clear.

But if you're writing a work of imagination, you *can* get stuck. Suddenly, in the middle of a novel or screenplay, you can find yourself unsure of where to go next. Even if you've armed yourself with a fairly rigorous outline, it's easy to come up against a wall. And the more you try to press on through that wall, the more your head hurts, until you give up. In despair.

But take heart. Maybe the reason you're stuck is a *good* one. While it could just be low blood sugar, it could also be a signal of something more significant. If *you're* not sure what happens next, then maybe *your reader* isn't sure, either. And that might be a good thing. It might mean that your narrative is crying out for something big at this point, some unexpected development, some shift in tone or jump in chronology. Your writer's block might not be a Stop sign, it might just be a Slow sign. It's telling you that more thought, rather than more typing, is required right now, that you've come to a kind of crossroads. Maybe something really exciting is about to happen, and it's simply going to take you some downtime to discover what that is.

But what if your block is so great that you can't even get started on *anything*? What if you approach your desk, kitchen table, or wherever you work, with the same joy you anticipate doing your taxes? That's a symptom of something deeper. While I'm not actually a psychiatrist (and am only playing one in this book), I think this kind of block has a lot to do with issues of self-worth. Even if you can't hear the actual words, you're asking yourself, *Who am I to be writing this book? What do I have to say that hasn't been said? And who would ever publish something I've composed?* You're leaping over everything else that has to come first—from sharpening your pencils to picking a name for your protagonist (much harder than you'd think) —and landing in a bramble bush of doubts and fears and negativity. But none of these things is truly a "writer's block"—they're a "living and breathing block," and maybe that's worse, but doing your work, any work, is ultimately going to prove your salvation. Achievement is the one thing that trumps depression, every time.

Writers who are blocked aren't incapable of writing—they can still hold a pen in their hand or sit at the keyboard. What they can't do is write as beautifully as they'd like, and that's what's stopping them. They put down three words, decide they're not Shakespeare, and tear them up. Do that enough times and you've got a very healthy block going. The eminent critic Jacques Barzun once wrote, "Convince yourself that you are working in clay, not marble, on paper, not eternal bronze; let that first sentence be as stupid as it wishes." And the second and third ones, too. "No one," Barzun added, "will rush out and print it as it stands." If you can accept that fact—and many blocked writers can't—you'll stop trying to write for the ages, and you'll start working instead on the humble, possibly disposable pages that most of us are fated to produce.

Most professional writers have a favorite form—short story, essay, play, novel—that they regularly employ to express themselves and their ideas. But every one of them moonlights now and then and uses a different form when the occasion calls for it.

So why shouldn't you?

Ideas come in all shapes and sizes, and sometimes what's right for a magazine article is all wrong for a nonfiction book. What might work fine as a screenplay may not have the heft for a novel. What might make for a lovely essay may not be translatable into fiction. And if, while trying to write one of these things, you keep getting hopelessly stuck, it might be because you've simply chosen the wrong form. It's the old round-peg-in-a-square-hole problem.

So what if, God forbid, your idea seems to want to become a play, and you've never written a play before? What if the short story threatens to swell into a novel? A lot of writers feel they either have to abandon the idea altogether or, first, spend several years studying the demands and requirement of the foreign form, buy every relevant book on the market, take every pertinent course—maybe even enroll in a university program and get a degree in it! If you happen to know that you are immortal, go right ahead—you've got all the time in the world.

For the rest of us, however, it's not that easy.

We hope to write, and even publish, our work in the span of a normal human lifetime. And we cannot become experts in

LoseYour Form

everything. Which is why it's important to remind ourselves that we already know a lot more than we think we do. For one thing, if your idea is begging to take shape as a play, then that may be because you've seen some plays (I bet you have!) and you can already imagine, albeit imprecisely, how this idea would work on the stage. By the same token, you've seen a lot of movies, which may be why your inner voice is insisting that something about this new idea of yours would lend itself neatly to the big screen.

Writers, to quote Cynthia Ozick, breathe "inside a blaze of words," and that's what makes them writers. Some of these words they have read in poems, some they have heard declaimed on Broadway, some have even been absorbed just from watching TV. (Yes, it is possible.) And whether the writers were aware of it or not, they were also imbibing the form the words were embodied in. Drinking the wine, they could not fail to notice the bottle from which it was being poured. When a new form beckons to you, when you feel that tingle of excitement, mixed with trepidation, which comes from accepting a challenge, rise to it—don't run away. I'm not suggesting you fly blind, that you take *no* time to comprehend the strictures of the new form, but I am suggesting that a lifetime spent in that blaze of words has left you far better prepared than you know.

Set an Alarm Clock.

While you're at it, set two.

One to make sure that you get to your desk on time every day; writing only gets harder the longer you stay away. And set the other one ticking in your work. When you're constructing a plot, see if you can't install, somewhere deep in the heart of the machinery, a little ticking clock that's counting down, second by second, to a big showdown of some sort.

Screenwriters live and die by this rule, which is why you see so many stories where the cop has to find the killer before the next full moon, or the heroine has to convince her old boyfriend to break off his imminent wedding, or the scientists have to figure out how the planet Earth can avoid the asteroid due to collide with it in just thirty-six hours! But screenwriters are definitely on to something here. That ticking clock can add immeasurably to any imaginative work.

For one, it gives your story a thrust, a spine, a destination. You can always check your progress against the looming cataclysm or unavoidable event. Are your readers worrying about the big tennis tournament your heroine has got to win? The declaration of love she must make before it is too late? The deadly conspiracy she must uncover and foil before the world, as we know it, is lost?

Because if they're not, they should be.

And are you, the author, ratcheting up the action and the ante? Are you using that clock like a time bomb, ready to explode? Have you set in motion a sequence of events that inevitably, and with increasing tempo, will lead to a critical juncture, one where the central conflict of your story will be resolved, for better or for worse? Also called a climax, every good story should have one. And when you build that climax in, you have all the advantages conferred by advance planning—you can see it coming, you can plan everything else to contribute to it, and you can prep your audience so they fully comprehend and appreciate the gravity of the event when you get them there. They'll know exactly how much is at stake—a lot!—and if you've done your job right, they'll be anxiously awaiting the outcome.

They should be watching the action like the dropping of the ball in Times Square on New Year's Eve —riveted, shivering, and drunk with expectation.

RULE 54. Fall in Love.

Before embarking on any substantial writing project,
ask yourself this: Am I in love?

Because if you're not in love with your subject, you will have a very hard time
seeing it through to completion.

If it's just some casual flirtation, you'll never be able to go the distance. You'll get tired, bored, restless. Something else will beckon to you, you'll chase after that instead, and the whole mad cycle will start all over again. (Ask yourself: Where is Hugh Hefner's *Remembrance of Things Past*?) Some projects may appeal to you because they are timely, or hot, or overtly commercial, and while there's nothing wrong with pursuing such stuff, it's never easy to maintain the necessary enthusiasm for them over the months, even years, that they can demand. Cheap thrills don't last.

Ah, but if it's true love, if the subject is one that truly speaks to your heart, then somehow you will find the will and the energy to see the project through to completion. If it's a story that you need to tell, then you'll find a way to tell it, no matter how many drafts you have to go through to get there. If it's a dream you want to share with the world, you'll find a way to make that happen.

And you will subscribe, as you must, to the theory of delayed gratification. Writing big things, like novels, biographies, and screenplays, means working, sometimes for years, just to get the thing done. And then there's the wait to see the work go out into the world as a book or a movie. Be forewarned: These are not quick turnaround industries—movies take a long time to set up, shoot, and distribute; books take a long time to get sold, printed, and shipped. I recently learned, for instance, that my new, finished novel—all done and in need of next to no editing, according to the publisher—will come out exactly nineteen months from now. Was I happy to hear it? No. But I've been around this track before, and I know that it's pointless to get agitated about it. The only thing to do is to start in on the next big project, to fall in love all over again, with something new and let those nineteen months pass—as, experience tells me, they do.

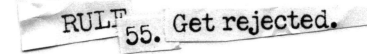

RULE 55. Get rejected.

**Into every writer's life, some rain must fall—
though sometimes it may feel more like a deluge.**

You will send your work out—to agents, editors, publishers—
and it will come back to you like a boomerang. Turned down,
passed on, rejected.

It's a rite of passage, and the sooner you make your peace
with it, the better off you'll be.

That's not saying you'll ever entirely get used to it. It's always
a shock when somebody doesn't love your work. And it's easy
to take it to heart—it feels like they're rejecting you, personally,
and not the work. But they're not (unless, in fact, they *do*
know you and for some reason you really *have* ticked them off).
No, when your work is rejected, that's all that's happening here,
and it could have been rejected for a whole host of reasons that
had nothing to do with the quality of the work itself. Your
project might have conflicted with something else they already
had in the pipeline, it might have been too long or too short for
their needs, it might have simply struck the wrong tone for their
market or audience. They might even be planning to go out of
business in three months, though they haven't gone public with
that information yet.

So whatever kind of rejection slip you get, don't waste a lot
of time trying to read anything into it. If it's a form rejection,
it's a form rejection, and that's that. But even if it's personal-
ized somehow, don't knock yourself out parsing every word and
figuring out what the editor meant. Most of the time she didn't
mean much; she was just trying to soften the blow.

But there's an old Jewish saying that's relevant here: "If one person says you look tired, shrug it off. If two people say you look tired, lie down." The same goes for rejection letters. If one editor says your manuscript is wrong for some reason, that could just be her opinion. But if a second editor mentions the exact same thing, give the complaint some serious thought. I sent out a partial manuscript of a novel once, and when the first editor passed on it because it seemed "cartoony" to her, I laughed it off. What did she know? But imagine my consternation when another editor, at a different house, also passed on it, saying it reminded her, uncomfortably, "of a cartoon." Now, unless these two had had lunch and discussed it, which seemed extremely unlikely, I had to concede that there just might be something vaguely cartoonish about it, after all. (Could it have been because the antagonist bore a strong resemblance to the Hulk?)

Rejection letters are a blow to even the strongest ego, but they can teach you a few things, besides humility. They can show you where your work isn't working, where you need to concentrate your creative fire, and what you might have to do to leap that final hurdle into publication.

But I don't care how many times you hear about writers who're so cool and confident that they festoon their walls with their rejection slips— I say read 'em, and then *throw them out!*

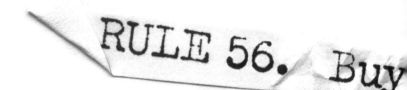

RULE 56. Buy

One of the sticks with which aspiring writers are most often hit over the head is, "Do you want to write ... or do you just want to be a writer?"

You're supposed to be chastised by that. Real writers, you're to understand, want to write; they *need* to write. Phonies just think about sitting around in comfy armchairs, being interviewed about what they've already written, surrounded by leather-bound collections of their work, a faithful dog, and a worshipful spouse.

To which I say, what's wrong with that? What's wrong with having a picture in your head of yourself as an accomplished and successful writer?

We all have to have some goal we're striving for, some idea of what we're aiming at, and the image of yourself basking in the glory and accolades is as good as any.

What, pray tell, is the alternative?

Should you imagine yourself, day after day, year after year, toiling over a cluttered desk, or wrestling a new ink cartridge into your printer? (If you're using an ink-jet, by the way, please consider getting a laser printer instead. It's better in the long run.) What kind of a fantasy is that? How is that supposed to get, and keep, you motivated?

.he Smoking Jacket.

No, I say go right ahead and dream away. Color in every square inch of your private fantasy. Savor every detail. No writer focuses on the image of himself writing any more than a bus driver dreams—except in his nightmares—of driving a bus.

Yes, you have to do the work, and yes, you *will* do it; that's a given. Writing—though it can be rewarding and even, on a good day, fun—is hard work, and no one would want to dwell on it too much.

Consider this fantasizing as a kind of self-actualization. (Now we're talking!) By concentrating on the end, not the means, you may be able to keep some of the troubles and doubts at bay. Thinking about your writing tends to become thinking about the *problems* in your writing. Thinking about flying to Stockholm to collect your Nobel Prize tends to become … wonderful. Thinking about syntax and structure will keep you up all night, while thinking about tuxedos and limousines will put you to sleep with a smile on your face.

And nothing will help you write better than a good night's rest.

RULE 57,
Keep Your Day Job.

As enjoyable as fantasizing can be—and I devote a healthy two or three hours a day to it myself—it's also important to be realistic about your writing. Especially when it comes to money.

In one of my classes, a female banker was determined to pin me down on the subject of her royalties. Even though she hadn't actually written or sold her book yet, she wanted to know how soon she could quit her job at the bank and start living off her writing income. When I explained, as I often have to do, that royalties are like quarks ("We theorize that they exist, but we never actually see them"), she was not amused. Some writers are so focused on the bottom line that they forget to pay enough attention to what they have to do first. Namely, write.

We all read in the papers about the monster deals made by writers like J.K. Rowling and Nicholas Sparks and James Patterson. But those deals are in the paper *because* they're such big news—and so rare. Most writers labor in obscurity, for far less money. The writers who make their fortunes the first time out of the gate, like Charles Frazier and *Cold Mountain*, are one in a million. It's all about as reliable as the lottery.

But if what you want to do is improve your chances of seeing a check in the mail, there are a few things you should know. One is that nonfiction sells more easily than fiction. Newspapers and magazines have a bottomless craving for news stories, features, trend pieces, profiles, travel essays, and humor columns. They don't just want these things, they *need* them, or else they're going to have to run blank pages in between all the ads they've already sold.

Publishers want nonfiction, too. The commercial viability of a nonfiction proposal, or manuscript, is much easier for them to assess than a novel. They can gauge how big an audience exists for your book idea and how many of these potential customers are likely to come out and buy it. If you've got a great new idea for a book about dieting, relationships, or careers, then they want to hear from you.

If, on the other hand, you have a novel, they may—or may not—want to hear from you. Publishers are always looking for the next big blockbuster (or the next writer capable of churning one out), but they're also very gun-shy. Most novels they buy don't do very well, so they're reluctant to invest much time or money, particularly in newcomers. They buy warily, promote stingily, and publish with little fanfare. Short-story collections are even harder to sell; if that's what you're interested in writing, your best bet is to start selling them to small literary magazines and gradually build a reputation that will catch the attention of a book editor or publishing house.

One screenwriter I know, lamenting the boom-or-bust nature of the writing life, put it nicely when he said, "You can get rich at this, but you just can't make a living."

Keep the day job until you can deposit your big, fat advance from the big, fat publishing house—and even then, wait three days for the check to clear.

RULE 58.
Pick a Personage.

If writing is, at its most fluent,
a form of talking, then the question you have to ask yourself is,
Who's doing the talking?

It's either you, in the first person—as in "I took my leave of the gendarmes"—or it's you in some variation of the third person—as in "Maurice took his leave of the gendarmes." (It could be you in the second person, I suppose—as in "You take your leave of the gendarmes"—but to pull that off at any length, you'd have to be Jay McInerney, who made the technique famous in *Bright Lights, Big City*. Nearly everyone who tried it afterward failed miserably.)

So, it's either going to be first or third, and in both instances, of course, it's going to be you behind the curtain, doing the talking for everybody. It's your writing, and you're creating everything on the page. But have you chosen the right voice to do it in?

When you're really planning to whale away, the first person is your ticket. It's the closest you'll get to your own voice. (Your writing voice is always, no matter what you do, going to be one shade off of your spoken voice, if only because it's an edited and shaped version of the original.) In a sustained narrative the first person solves a lot of problems for you. If "I" am telling the story, then it's only what *I* know, and *I* see, and *I* hear, that I can relate. It's easy to maintain the focus, and the intensity, of the story and at the same time forge an intimate bond with the reader. That's probably why a lot of antiheroes use it; it's hard for the reader to hate someone who's been whispering so openly and confidingly in his ear.

But what if the first person isn't working for you? It happens a lot, and usually it's because the material is so close to you, so personal and revealing, that the same impulse that originally drove you to write in the first person is now warning you to back off, to cool down, to conceal some things. You're growing uncomfortable with owning up to what's on the page.

And that's true even if the first-person narrator is someone else, someone you've made up entirely. I don't care if you're lurking behind a character named Englebert or Brunhilda—sometimes that "I" can feel too restricting, and too close, and you can't quite shake feeling identified with it somehow. Worse, you can't help thinking that readers are going to confuse the two of you—author and character—somehow.

That's when you might want to think about shifting your narrative to the third person. Try writing the same pages in the third person and see if that doesn't free you up. Sometimes all you need is to change "I'd been happily married for ten years and yet felt irresistibly drawn to this mysterious stranger" to "Alex had been happily married for ten years and yet felt irresistibly drawn to this mysterious stranger." One will have your mother calling to find out what's wrong in your marriage, and the other will have the Lifetime network calling to buy the story rights.

RULE 59.

Ham It Up.

The one place where the first-person point of view was traditionally verboten was journalism.

If you were a reporter, writing for a newspaper or magazine, you were strongly advised, if not downright forbidden, ever to say "I" or to refer to yourself in the story. If you had to, it was under such strange locutions as "this reporter" or the editorial "we," for which the *New Yorker* "Talk of the Town" pieces were so well known—and so often mocked. ("We were delighted to attend the pointillist exhibition at the Academy of the Arts, where we enjoyed cucumber sandwiches cut to precisely the right size.")

And in some quarters, little has changed. If you're writing for the front page of the *New York Times*, you are probably going to be limited to official, objective journalese, and the only indication that you personally are doing the reporting will be your byline at the top of the story. But guess what? If it's the *New York Times*, that's plenty!

But in many other quarters, things have gotten a lot looser. With the advent of what is called everything from "creative journalism" to "literary nonfiction" to the "literature of fact," writers have been allowed, if not encouraged, to sneak themselves into the story and on camera. And yet, even though that privilege has been proffered, many writers have been loathe to accept it. Either they are too timid to exploit the opportunity or too confined by previous expectations and long-standing rules to take advantage of this big chance. And even when they do, they limit themselves to innocuous observations or unrevealing asides.

Sometimes the material is so lively and engaging it speaks for itself, but many times it's not—and that's when a bold, opinionated, authorial voice can save the day. Many times, all a piece of nonfiction writing needs to jazz it up is a loud, strong intrusion from the writer herself! What were your personal feelings about your subject? What surprised you, bothered you, pleased you ... *personally*? Was the staff at the ultrafabulous resort you checked into too ultrafabulous to get the right bags to your room? Or did you perhaps have some unusual interaction with one of the people in the piece? (A rock star who shared with you a tour of his rare-book collection? A prima ballerina you caught snarfling down a bag of pork rinds? A nuclear physicist who wanted nothing more than to play a round of Clue?)

> **By putting yourself into the story—not necessarily at its center, but there, present and accounted for, nonetheless—you can add zest and color and, above all, immediacy, to even the driest of topics.**

RULE 60.

Know No Shame.

Of the many privileges afforded a writer, perhaps the one I cherish most is the right to be nosy.

If you're a writer, you get to ask anybody just about anything. You get to pull out your pad (you are carrying one now, right?) and fire away at anyone. "What first got you interested in building an atomic reactor in your yard? How exactly do you find your fissionable material? Is your wife an enthusiast, too?" Although, in a case like this, your next call might be to the Department of Homeland Security, in most such instances you'll be dialing up an editor to pitch the fascinating story you've just stumbled across.

Writers are not only entitled to be inquisitive, they're required to be. If you're not interested in what the people around you are doing, and why they're doing it, then you're probably not destined to write for newspapers or magazines. In fact, you're probably not suited to writing fiction, either, because what makes most fiction work is its characters. Aside from certain best-sellers that, to my mind, have only cardboard characters being put through their assigned paces by an author more interested in plot than people (I mention no names), good novels and short stories are populated by characters whose complex personalities and motivations drive the story and make the book impossible to put down.

Take a novel I recently read, Ian McEwan's *Atonement*. In the first half of this book, almost nothing happens. Really. An aristocratic family assembles at a country house, a letter is mis-delivered, and an impressionable girl sees some things she's too young to understand. But from just such unpromising stuff, a book of immense drama and portent has been fashioned. And it's all because the author has, plainly, studied people, how they conduct themselves, and why they do what they do.

In the best sense of the words, if there is one, McEwan is both a voyeur and an eavesdropper—and an expert one at that.

Writers have to be a bit of both. They have to understand the nuances, the elisions, the confessions and confusions that make life the unpredictable mess it is. They must grow to observe with fastidious attention the subtle signals with which people communicate their desires and their needs and listen, with equal care, to the way they express, or avoid, those same longings. When interviewing people, you have to be as alive to their expressions, their gestures, their general deportment as you are to the words your tape recorder is capturing. It's only when you put the two together that you get, and can give, the full picture.

To write well, about anything,
you must have curiosity in your nature.
To write well about people or characters,
you have to be downright shameless.

RULE 61

Pass the Scuttlebutt.

And while we're cultivating the negative virtues, another thing writers should be is gossips.

There is no greater source of information in this world—easily surpassing the Library of Congress, the Encyclopaedia Britannica, and the World Wide Web, combined—than simple, old-fashioned "you're not going to believe this!" gossip.

Gossip is the way we learn all the really important stuff. It's how we learn who's sleeping with whom, who's making more money than we are, who our true friends and secret enemies are. Gossip is a kind of interpersonal barter, a money-less exchange where we get to trade nuggets of information. *I'll tell you what went down after the party ended if you tell me why Cindy won't look me in the eye anymore.* To get the good stuff in return, you have to have something to give up; otherwise, people stop trading with you. Good gossip is valuable and everybody expects a quid pro quo.

As a writer, you want to be sure to have a ready stock on hand; that way, you'll always be able to pick up more. But why do you want it? That's easy. You want it because gossip is the unofficial version of events; it's the private face of public affairs. Gossip fills in all the gaps, explains all the motivations, charts all the currents. It's the common coin of human commerce, and no writer can ever have enough of it.

Whether you're trying to create complex characters for a story or write a nuanced profile of a public figure, you're going to have to rely on what you know of human nature, what you've come to understand about how we all really behave and why we do the things we do. The official version of events seldom covers that. We learn about people from other people, from talking to them, swapping stories and opinions, jokes and observations.

We also learn about ourselves; one of the greatest virtues of gossip is that it gives us a chance, in a casual, nonjudgmental format, to check our own proclivities and attitudes against everybody else's. *Is it wrong to make out in the copy room? Do other people chisel a bad waiter on the tip? Does anyone else forget his parents' birthdays?* As writers, we're always trying to decide if we're crazy or not (generally, the answer is yes), but gossip is a good way to find out.

RULE 62.

It's easy to accept the acceptable,
to applaud the laudable.

But it's quite another to accept the *un*acceptable, to find in ourselves the capacity to understand, and even forgive, conduct and behavior we regard as reprehensible or worse. For writers, that's where the going gets rough.

And interesting.

If, instead of stereotyping people or portraying them with a few slapdash effects, we can fully imagine them and enter into the world *as they perceive it*, then we've gone right through the looking glass and into the heart and soul of the character. If we can suspend our personal judgment and see things as they do, feel things as they feel them, then we've managed to go where few writers ever do.

It's one reason artists are drawn to the challenge of presenting the unpresentable, of delving into the seamy, the sordid, the morally offensive. Sure, it makes for good material—who wants to read about a bunch of goody-goodies all the time—but it also forces the writer to raise his game. Can you dig deep enough to find the common humanity? Can you identify, vicariously, with even the most shocking desires, and make them comprehensible

Go Inside.

to your audience? Your readers don't have to like your characters—heck, you probably don't like them yourself—but if you've made your audience feel what it is to be inside their skin, you've done your job, and then some.

The same holds true for nonfiction. Interview a bigot and it's easy as pie to make him look and sound ridiculous—but, once published, the interview is just as easily dismissed and forgotten. What did you tell us that we didn't already know or that your subject hadn't made clear in his own words? Nothing. But if you could drop your defenses, as it were, if you could open yourself up and simply see things through your subject's eyes, it's possible that you could come back with something truly revealing—maybe even something constructive. How did he get that way? What experiences shaped him? How have his perceptions become so skewed? Come up with answers to questions like these and you might even keep such weeds from springing up elsewhere.

Must you become some crusader on a mission? Hardly. But practicing empathy, a kind of divine omniscience and benign acceptance, can help you to get the story—and it can also help you to find the real story, the one lying just below. The one that shows us not just what happened (that's usually the easy part) but *why* it did.

RULE 63.
De-claim!
De-Claim!

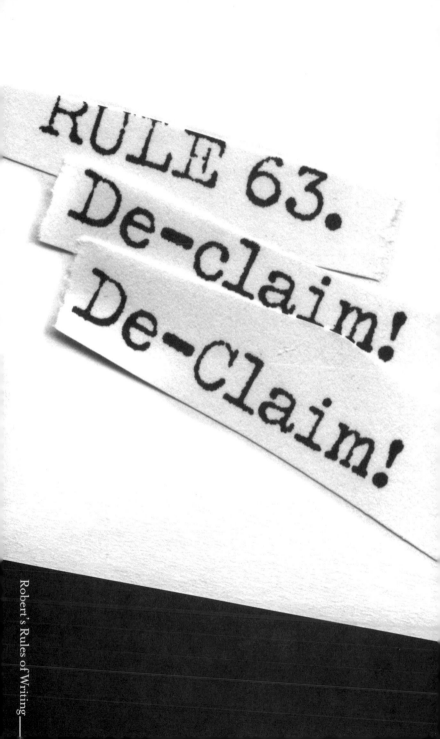

With the surge in cell phone use these days,

it's gotten a lot harder to know who's crazy anymore.

At one time, if you saw somebody talking to himself on the street, it was a dead giveaway. But that is no longer the case.

Which is good news for writers.
One more professional tic has become less noticeable.

Talking to yourself is the best way, in my book, to iron out all the last stubborn wrinkles in your prose. What looks perfectly good on the page—smooth and streamlined and effortless— may not sound so good when you actually try to utter it aloud. Dialogue you thought was clever and punchy may sound elliptical and baffling when you act it out; sometimes you may even discover that certain lines can't be said without running out of breath. And narrative passages that seemed downright poetic when you wrote them may come off as overblown, purple, and pompous; if you inexplicably find yourself orating them with an English accent, then that should tell you something right there. But you don't have to be a thespian of the first order to reap the benefits of reading aloud. All you have to do is close the door to your office (no point in alarming other members of the household) and softly, but audibly, pronounce the words you've written.

Where do you stumble? Where do you momentarily lose the sense of what you're saying? Where do you find the same words recurring too often? Do you, at some point, lose the easy thread of your own prose?

The thing to keep in mind is that all writing is written to be spoken aloud, even if that means in absolute silence under the nose of the scariest librarian. You're asking your reader to *hear* the words, if only in her own head, and respond to them accordingly. You're asking that same reader, if your work includes quotations or speaking parts, to assume those roles and hear those lines, too, as you have written them. You've provided a lot of clues, in the specific words you've chosen and in the artful way you have chosen to deploy them. But if the words don't ring true when you try them out, then they will surely ring wrong in the more strictly enforced privacy of a reader's skull.

RULE 64.
Take the Long Way.

Speaking of a reader's skull, let me just say that there's a lot more room in there than you might imagine.

We all hear a lot these days about the shrinking attention span of the American public. Corrupted by TV commercials, movie trailers, computer games, and music videos in which the images stream by at the speed of light, we are all supposedly incapable of holding a thought for more than a minute without reaching for the remote.

And yet, books that weigh a ton keep right on selling.

Stephen King, Anne Rice, Tom Clancy, Dan Brown—none of them can be accused of going light on the typewriter. Historical tomes and hefty biographies, from fine writers like David McCullough, James MacPherson, and Niall Ferguson, never fail to find an enthusiastic reception. And whether or not

you think these books
could actually use a bit of judicious pruning,
they are clearly satisfying a large audience just the way they are.

Nothing encourages me more.

Readers, or at least an awful lot of them, are still embracing full-bodied books, books that don't stint on anything. Novels with large casts of characters, complex plots that cover long spans of time or traverse whole continents. That's what books can do, like nothing else can. And people are still turning to them for just that reason.

Writers, as a result, need never hold back. If in your novel you want to flashback to your heroine's youth and show some incidents from her formative years, go right ahead—and if you want to stay there for a hundred pages, feel free. True, you have to make that material interesting, and I'm not saying your book should be padded, but you don't have to hold back because you think your readers may not be able to handle it. They can handle anything you throw at them and, truth be told, many readers (and I'd have to number myself among them) enjoy a big, fat wallow. When I choose a book to read, I am also choosing a world in which I plan to immerse myself for some time. It's one reason I don't cotton so much to short stories—reading a short story makes me feel like I just got wet and already I have to get out of the bath. A big book is like a sunken tub, and once I'm in, and the water's hot, I like to loll around in there.

Whether it's a
political biography
or a multigenerational saga,

let your narrative unfold in as lush
and deliberate a manner as you choose.

If it's interesting to you, then there's a very good chance it will be interesting to others, too. Who would have thought that the story of a long-forgotten racehorse would grip millions of readers? I doubt that even Laura Hillenbrand, who wrote *Seabiscuit*, had expectations that high. But breakout books like that just go to show that readers—good readers—are willing to follow the right writer almost anywhere.

RULE 65.   Show No Mercy.

Writers don't write, I was repeatedly told at my first magazine job in New York, they *rewrite*.

Every time I heard it I wanted to weep.

And I didn't believe it. Every time I did have to rewrite something, I took it as a sign that I wasn't really very good at this, and that I should start looking for a more suitable line of work at my earliest opportunity.

Truth be told, I still think that what flows from my keyboard should be so pristine that it allows for no further improvement. To this day I can't understand why it's not … but at least, in a small sign of progress, I *do* understand that it's not.

Writing is a process—of discovery, of refinement, of invention.

The notion that you can just bang it out in immaculate condition is worse than arrogant, it's positively self-destructive. First of all, you'll give yourself a complex thinking that all the other writers out there are turning out perfect prose while you're not. And second, you'll fail to do what needs to be done to make your work as good as it could, and should, be.

William Faulkner, in an oft-quoted remark, said, "You've got to kill all your darlings," and while I think that may be a bit of

an overstatement—surely *some* of your darlings can be spared—
I take his general point. You have to be ruthless in the service
of the work. Many times the very thing that sparked your
imagination, that got you writing this particular piece in
the first place, will turn out to be, by the time you're done,
irrelevant or beside the point. There's even a chance that it
will have been superseded by something better, more apposite,
which only occurred to you while writing. Most good things
occur to you not while you're *thinking* about writing but while
you're actually doing it. This is something that legions of
would-be writers never grasp; they claim that they've composed
entire stories, novels, and clever essays but that so far, tapping
their foreheads with one finger, the pages all still "up here."
It's just a matter of finding the time, they say, to put everything
down on paper. (Only they never get around to doing it, do
they?)

Great writing is seldom written;
it's rewritten, and yes, the ink is usually diluted with blood, sweat, tears,
and way too much Diet Coke.

RULE 66
Doubt Everyone.

Writing can be a lonely task, and one way that a lot of writers in Hollywood have gotten around that problem is by becoming a team—especially when it comes to writing comedy. Having somebody else in the room with you, particularly when it comes to trying out comedic banter, is a big help. If both of you laugh, it's a keeper. If neither one of you laughs, it's back to the drawing board.

In the greater world, many writers turn to local writing groups, where several writers get together every week, or maybe every month, to share their work and offer critiques and encouragement. And while I think the encouragement part is nice—helpful and soul-sustaining—there is also a risky downside.

Whenever your work comes out for a public airing, it runs the risk of getting diluted. Everybody in the writing group is going to have an opinion, and while some of these comments might be useful and on point, others won't. Will you always be able to distinguish between them? Especially when you are in the middle of composition? What if somebody had told Beethoven that starting the *Fifth Symphony* with three straight Gs was boring? What if somebody told Proust that a madeleine was a lousy idea, and it would be better to focus on a tasty ragout?

What if someone had told Victor Hugo his ending for *The Hunchback of Notre Dame* was too downbeat, and why *couldn't* Quasimodo and Esmerelda just find a way to make it work together?

Even the most well-intentioned advice can be distracting, if not destructive. I have personally witnessed fresh and original work get mauled in a group discussion and seen the writer leave with the impression that he should come up with something more predictable and in keeping with the group consensus. It's easy to be swayed, especially if more than one person is clamoring in your ear. Who among us has 100 percent confidence in his work?

Democracy is nice when it comes to government, but in the arts it is awfully fallible. Van Gogh couldn't sell his paintings, Manet was reviled by the academy, Melville starved, Stravinsky's *Rite of Spring* was booed, John Kennedy Toole couldn't get *A Confederacy of Dunces* published until he was dead, J.P. Donleavy's *The Ginger Man* was rejected dozens of times and has since been voted one of the best one hundred books of the last century. I could go on for days.

And don't even get me started on editors and agents. Because of their professional status, their opinions take on extra weight. I had one agent who routinely vetoed my nonfiction book ideas, telling me they were "articles, not books." And I believed him, until I started noticing that six months to a year later, these same ideas were showing up as other people's books. I may have been behind the curve a bit, but I was *not* out to lunch. Magazine editors, too, have often taken a pass on feature ideas of mine that later turned up elsewhere, in some very similar incarnation. I'm not blaming them, they're only human, but I am saying that they don't always *know*.

If you're going to listen to other people's opinions—whether it's by joining a writing group, consulting with an agent, or pitching to an editor—proceed with caution. Remember at all times that there is only one opinion that matters in the end, and that's yours.

Find Your Ideal

RULE 67.

For those who don't wish to keep their writing under close wraps, hermetically sealed until ready for immediate publication, there is a compromise solution.

And that would be your ideal reader.

Although writing groups can prove dangerous, so can writing in total secrecy. You may be a writer who *needs* to check in with the world now and then and have some validation of the work you're doing. You may *want* to have the occasional course corrective or constructive (if you can find it) criticism. You may need to air your prose and get some idea of how the world will react to the finished work. And for that, you need a sounding board.

Which is easier said than found.

You need to find someone at least as intelligent as yourself (and Lord *knows* how hard that is!). But wedded to this intelligence must be an innate sense of diplomacy.

Your reader must be a good enough friend to tell you the truth but so sensitive to your moods and attitude that the truth is delivered in a safe, benign, and tactful manner. Already we're approaching the realm of the impossible.

Should your ideal reader be a writer herself? A fellow writer may be better at pinpointing the problems and possible solutions; you can really talk craft, nuts-and-bolts stuff, with someone who's been there, too.

But a civilian can give you the kind of John Q. Public reaction that generally matters the most. What will the everyday reader make of your work? Will it find an audience in the great beyond?

The decision is up to you. For years, my own ideal reader was another writer, Linda, who lived exactly equidistant from a Greek diner, called the Silver Star, where we could get together, with a menu featuring the foods of all nations, to offer each other advice and counsel. The fact that we were both writers made for a nicely reciprocal arrangement.

But oddly enough, even though I now live three thousand miles away from Linda, and we talk no more than every other month, she is still in some sense my ideal reader. When I write something funny, I find myself thinking, "Would Linda laugh?" When I'm writing something sober, I think, "Would Linda approve?" Or would she highlight—oh so gently—some problem I hadn't seen? Whether physically present, marking up your manuscript, or spiritually hovering, whispering suggestions in your ear, your ideal reader is a version of your highest self, forcing you to strive for the best you can do. For instance, no matter how much you don't want to do that fourteenth rewrite, if your ideal reader keeps pushing for it, do it.

RULE 68.

Your blood is boiling. Your dander is up. You can hardly wait to start writing. In fact, you're not going to wait another second! You're going to sit down and scrawl the immortal words, the timeless thoughts that are coursing through your veins like fire—*God, doesn't it feel good to get it all out!*—before you lose an ounce of the passion you're feeling right now. Isn't that what all the writing books and instructors are always telling you to do: Write out of passion?

Be my guest—write out of all the passion you can manage— but just **don't expect it to be very good.**

Passion, whether it's anger or indignation, love or lust, hatred or sorrow, is wonderful fuel, burning hot and burning bright, but it's also burning out of control. When you're in the throes of these emotions, you're not thinking all that clearly, and you're probably not writing that way, either. You're pouring it all out on the page, raw, unrefined, unmediated, and unmediated upon. It's like going on a crying jag—cathartic, draining, and ultimately a relief. For you.

But not necessarily for the reader.

Passion has a way of clouding the judgment (ever fall madly in love with somebody who wasn't really right for you?) and it has a way of muddying up prose, too. The immortal Oscar Wilde wrote a deeply passionate prison letter, *De Profundis*, to his erstwhile lover, Lord Alfred Douglas, but even he went on and on, around and around in circles, mixing up all kinds of clever insights and fine turns of phrase (he wasn't Oscar Wilde for nothing!) with vast swatches of bathos and repetitive twaddle. And for all his self-flagellation, Wilde went right back to his toxic lover as soon as he was released from jail—which just goes to show that even genius can't see straight when passion enters the picture.

What you feel strongly, and strongly about, is of course great material from which to mine your future work—and write it all down, as you feel it, as freely as you like. But regard it as the ore, not the finished work, that it is. Even a newspaper editorial, written with all the heat and haste you felt overwhelm you in the act of composition, needs to cool off overnight. The next day you'll be surprised to see that, for all its energy, it's not perhaps as persuasive, or even as coherent, as it could be. It may seem, even to you, its author, intemperate. (So you can only imagine how it would strike the average reader.) By and large, writing with a little less passion, and a little more polish, serves everyone a lot better.

RULE 69.

Grumble and Fuss.

Years ago I was at a dinner party in Chicago where one of the other guests, a local author, leaned back in his chair and declared, "I've never written a word that I'm not proud of." A general silence fell, followed by the obligatory murmur of appreciation. What else could you do?

And I suppose you could say that it's nice he was proud of every word he's ever written; Martha Stewart would say that's a good thing. After all, who would want to be ashamed of his own work? Who would want to have to deny it in public: "That rubbish, with *my* name on it? Must be a mistake—I never saw the stuff in my life."

But at the same time, it made me suspicious then, and it makes me suspicious now. I don't really know many satisfied writers—in fact, apart from that guy, I don't think I know any—and that seems to me to be about right. Writers *should* be unsatisfied with their work. It's part of our job description.

Writers tend to be obsessive creatures; we live much of the time in our own heads, where we make the rules and where we have only illusory playmates to join in the planned activities. Anybody who misbehaves can be banished, instantly. We are born autocrats.

But we are also our own worst enemies. Every sentence, every word, every syllable sometimes gets the once-over, and what seems fine to us today looks wretched to us tomorrow.

And appalls us when it's finally in print.

Writers reading their own work seldom see all the good stuff, and when they do, they usually gloss over it. What they see instead are the passages that rattle badly, the paragraphs that begin with a whimper, the humorous asides that fall flat. They hear the verbal echoes they can't believe they didn't hear before, they see the gaps where a necessary connection should have been made, the fine flourishes that look more like silly frippery now.

Like actors who claim to hate watching themselves on screen, writers often hate to read their own work. (But we mean it.)

> Oblivious to the merits, alert to the faults, we find it less than an enjoyable experience. But that inveterate dissatisfaction is what marks us as writers in the first place. If you want to write, you want to get it right—you worry over every word. And that worry, sorry to say, never really goes away. Every time something you wrote appears—in the newspaper, between book covers, on the movie screen—you will want to call out, "Hold it!" Why? Because you've just had a better idea; you've just seen a way to do it differently.
>
> But don't fret. Cherish your malcontent status, and remember: Only the bad writers are ever truly satisfied.

RULE 70.
Engage the Enemy.

Don't let anybody kid you: Both successful writers and unsuccessful writers procrastinate—it's as common as a computer glitch, and just as debilitating—but there is one big difference.

Successful writers get over it.

One of my best buddies in college was a guy we called Greenie—brilliant fellow, terrific writer (when he could be made to). But there was just something about a looming deadline that made Greenie put on the brakes. If a paper was due on a Tuesday, he couldn't be made to start it anytime sooner than Wednesday. While all the rest of us were grinding away on our theses—a yearlong project, necessary for graduation—Greenie was reading Sainte-Beuve, in French, for fun, and arguing about philosophy over endless cups of coffee in the student center.

During one of these conversations, Greenie asked me, in all seriousness, how I did it—how I kept my nose to the grindstone and actually arranged to turn things in when they were due. "I mean," he said in a spirit of inquiry and not admiration, "why do you do it?"

Hmm. I had to think about it, but eventually I came up with several reasons. For one thing, I'm compulsive by nature. For another, I fear censure and dread authority. A coward by nature, I weep when scolded.

But the real reason was more calculated than any of that, and it's just something I'd learned long before. If I put off writing a school paper until it was almost due, the leisure time, I discovered, wasn't really all that leisurely. I'd walk around feeling guilty and beleaguered, with a sense of pressure building up over my head like a massive thunderstorm.

This pressure only decreased, in an almost uncanny proportion, as the time I devoted to the work that was due increased.

In other words, the sooner I got down to work, the sooner the pressure let up. And the more I worked, the more that cloud hanging over my head dissipated. The calculation was a fairly simple one to make, and I never forgot it.

Procrastination doesn't make the task any sweeter or better, it just drags the whole thing out. Every day you delay makes the work look more formidable, and every day you chip away at it, even with only a few paragraphs, makes it look that much more manageable. Although I was never able to convince Greenie of this, wrestling the beast is, in the end, preferable to tiptoeing around it for weeks.

RULE 71.
Mix It Up

Ever take a long train trip, where you settled down into your seat, a good book in your lap, the wheels of the train rattling over the tracks, *clickety-clack, clickety-clack* ... only to wake up hours later in Delaware?

What lulled you into sleep was the gentle rocking of the cabin, the monotonous rhythm of the train barreling along at a steady clip, over the evenly spaced tracks, the soothing and regular predictability of it all.

But what you might enjoy in a railroad excursion is death when it comes to prose. You shouldn't fall asleep reading it, and you shouldn't fall asleep writing it.

In your work, you want to shake things up. You want to follow short sentences with long ones, florid passages with more straightforward stuff, action sequences with calmer bits, love scenes with explosions (literal or otherwise). The course of your narrative, like that of true love, should not run smooth. You want your train to screech along a hairpin turn now and then, to plunge into a black tunnel, to race along an open stretch of land, then slow to climb a long ascent ... before tearing back down again into a green valley.

Think Disneyland, not Amtrak.

How can you tell when your prose needs more variety? Well, first of all, if it's putting you to sleep, it's sure to put others to sleep as well. Give it the old audio test by reading it out loud. Hearing the words spoken is the easiest way to gauge their effect. Notice, in particular, if your breathing remains perfectly regular. Are you able to recite the words with a predictable beat? Do you, in fact, sort of know, at all times, just what's coming next? Is everything laid out as perfectly as a topiary garden? Are there no abrupt switches in rhythm, or from humor to pathos, from bold statement to subtle insinuation, from the matter-of-fact to the sublime?

Anytime you catch yourself falling into a singsong rhythm, much less glancing at your watch, you know things need a little pick-me-up, an alteration in tone or mood, or simply a change of scene. Imagine yourself at the throttle of the train, gazing out at the tracks ahead—is everything straight and level? Then imagine, just for the sake of variety, what else you might see out there. How might you wake up your snoozing passengers? By pulling back on the brakes? Pushing forward on the throttle? Or, at the very least, giving one long, loud, eardrum-shattering blast on the whistle?

Don't worry about alienating your readers—if they hadn't wanted to go for a ride, they would never have bought a ticket.

RULE 72.
Graph It.

Ever notice how magazines break up dense blocks of text with what is called in the business a pull-quote?

That's a quote from the article, reprinted in larger type than the rest, and giving the page, which would otherwise be nothing but unalleviated copy, a less forbidding appearance. It's a way to give the reader an occasional break, or oasis, for both his eye and his mind.

You should do the same when you're writing your own deathless prose. If all you see on the page is a block of words, with no indentations, no dialogue, no line breaks or subheads, you might want to look at the page again. Is it, really, all one thought? Is it all a single idea, one which does not allow for any natural pause or interruption?

Maybe it is. Maybe you are channeling, for our age, the spirit of Henry James, and your *Portrait of a Hottie* is destined to become a classic.

But in most instances, that one long, long paragraph you've got going is actually three or four paragraphs that have been shackled together like prisoners on a chain gang and are dragging each other along. And perhaps it's time to break the chain.

A nice little paragraph indentation is like an invitation to the reader to take a breath, to blink, to stop for a second to absorb the information that just preceded it, before starting in on the great new material to come. It also suggests that you have an order to your argument, or a design to your story. A great big lump of prose looks—fairly or not—undigested, while a paragraph structure looks deliberate and carefully planned. Maybe that's why Sue Williams, a friend of mine who's a lawyer, tells me she was taught never to write a legal brief in which a sentence was more than two lines long, or a page where there weren't at least three paragraphs. While, normally, I would never look to lawyers for advice on any kind of writing (I can't even understand the instructions on my jury summons), this strikes me as wise counsel.

Of course, *what* you're writing will also play a big part. If it's an academic paper, your paragraphs are probably going to be thicker and longer than they would if a question of tenure were not hanging in the balance; academics prize impenetrability.

But if you're writing a thriller, well, what could be more thrilling than pages that virtually turn themselves, where the story cascades down like a waterfall?

And if you're writing a comedic piece, what could be better than an abrupt halt now and then to deliver the punch line?

Newspaper stories, almost by definition, have a lot of short paragraphs; readers, it is understood, may be jouncing along in a subway car or trying to follow the story at a busy breakfast table. The reporter's got to fit his prose in between bites of toast or bus stops—which makes the paragraph his best friend, and yours, too.

RULE 73. Join Up.

And now I'd like to make a point.

It's perfectly okay to start a sentence, as above, with "And."

But you were taught never to do that? Then you were probably taught that you can't start a sentence with "But" either.

And that's untrue, too.

I've been doing both for years, ever since I started writing professionally and I was no longer in any danger of having an English teacher mark me down for it. (With only one exception, no editor—at a newspaper, magazine, or publishing house—has ever had a problem with it.) For me, both of these ways of starting a sentence always passed the natural speech test; that is, people naturally began their sentences with both conjunctions, and if it sounded perfectly okay to my ear, and made perfect sense to the other person, then it was good enough to be written that way, too.

For me, that's always been the bottom line: Does it sound right and communicate my meaning?

Writing is hard enough when you consider all the worthwhile rules that *are* worth observing. It becomes well nigh impossible when you have to worry about rules that exist simply because they've always *been* rules. And making your prose look—and sound—seamless means, among other things, using any conjunction you need, whenever you need it.

You want your sentences to flow, to meld into one another, to carry the reader along on an irresistible tide of narrative suspense, descriptive bravura, or rigorous logic. Sometimes the words and thoughts just connect effortlessly, segueing from one to another like a relay team passing the baton.

But at other times, you're going to need a conjunction, acting like a traffic cop, to signal the way ahead. When you say "Of course," you're usually about to make a sharp turn, as in "Of course, there are some politicians whose reputations are spotless." When you say "Furthermore," you're indicating that, to your mind, you've nailed down that last point and you're moving on to the next. When you say "Consequently," you're clearly claiming that what you're about to say proceeds incontestably from what you just said. Use these conjunctions wisely, and your readers will relax and go with the flow. Like tourists on a rafting trip, they'll trust you to handle the tiller and keep them safe and (relatively) dry.

RULE 74 Stake

I hate moving, but I love exploring my new neighborhood. I love taking a walk down unfamiliar blocks, thinking, "Why would anyone paint a house that color?" or, "Whose idea was it to put in that cactus garden?" And though I think I'll never get bored with these blocks, I inevitably do.

Within a few weeks, they become nothing more than the blocks I walk the dog down.

And if I had to write about them, it'd be hard. Even though I know them well, I don't really see them any longer. I can't figure out what would make them interesting to anyone because they're no longer interesting to me. My eye has grown cold.

Sometimes, when you're writing about something terribly familiar, you have to step back and try to imagine yourself into the shoes of someone who is not familiar with it. If it's your town, or your neighborhood, try to recall what you felt when you first saw it. What surprised or delighted you? What made you decide to move there (unless it was decided for you by the Witness Protection Program)? Now, think about how you feel when you're a tourist in a new city. You know how everything, from the pretzel carts to the statues in the park, seems new and novel and noteworthy? Well, that's how your town might look to somebody who's never been there. That's how it once looked to you.

Your Claim.

A new novel just came out, and it happens to take place on the campus of my alma mater—and in the very club of which I was a member. And what's most interesting about it to me is the way that the authors (two guys collaborated on the book) have written about my old stomping grounds. They've managed to bring it all back to me but at the same time show it to me in a new light. On the one hand, I'm impressed, and on the other, I'm annoyed. Strangely, it's a common writer's affliction to believe that everyplace he's been, everything's he's encountered, is territory that belongs to him, whether he's using it for anything or not, forever. Once in a while, it had occurred to me to set something on that college campus, but of course I'd never gotten around to it. Still, how dare these whippersnappers do it first? Have they no respect for their elders?

Stake your claim now. If something has been nagging at you, something that tells you to write about it, write about it now. Refresher courses are fine, but nothing beats a fresh eye.

RULE 75.
Get in
Style.

When you think of most successful writers, you think first of their subject matter. Anne Rice, and you think of vampires. Elmore Leonard, and you think of small-time crooks and scam artists. F. Scott Fitzgerald, and you conjure up the Jazz Age world of East Coast money and privilege.

But lots of writers have written about these same subjects—there are shelves of vampire books, tons of crime capers, and no shortage of stories about dissolute WASPs. So what, apart from their virtuoso storytelling, sets these writers apart and makes their work so much more memorable than the general run?

In a word, style. You could pick up a book by any one of these writers, and without even glancing at the cover, you'd know after reading a paragraph or two whose hands you were in. Anne Rice doesn't just tell spooky stories populated by witches and bloodsuckers, she writes in a lush, ornate style that creates a world of its own, a fever dream of sensuous detail, all evoked in a manner as indulgent and refined as her subject matter.

Elmore Leonard captures the down-market denizens of his world in a clipped, breezy style, one that manages to gently mock and strangely coddle them at the same time. You root for the losers snared in his seemingly effortless web.

And F. Scott, my own favorite? There's a music in his prose that no one else has ever been able to capture. While there are plenty of Hemingway contests ("Write the opening of a story in Hemingway's style, and win a trip to Harry's Bar!"), there is no such thing for Fitzgerald. Why? Because his style is too subtle for that, too soft and even elegiac. It'd be like trying to imitate a flute, not a tuba. From *The Great Gatsby*: "We are boats beating against the current, borne back ceaselessly into the past." How can you not love it?

To a great extent, **you don't pick your style at all — your style picks you.**

And that goes just as much for a historian or biographer as it does for a novelist or short-story writer. David McCullough, Edmund Morris, Simon Winchester—they all write with an inimitable and highly personal style, and even if they were to write about the very same figures or events, the accounts would wind up sounding entirely different and distinctive.

Unique as your fingerprints, your style is what enfolds your readers, what suffuses the air around them as they read, and in its many nuances conveys everything from mood to meaning.

RULE 76.

Change Your Spots.

But that's not to say your style can't be, shall we say … calibrated.

If you could write in only one style, as sturdy and unbending as a mighty oak, you would be limiting yourself in terms of the formats you could embrace, the markets you could approach, and the audiences you could reach. Has One Size Fits All ever fit anyone well?

Let's say you like to write in a casual, colloquial style. That may work beautifully for short essays and newspaper articles, but it may not work for the big, important family history on which you feel compelled to embark. (Think hard about that decision, by the way.) Yes, you can still use your customarily graceful touch, but a style that's as light as air may not allow you the gravitas you feel your book will require.

Conversely, you may prefer a fairly weighty delivery; maybe you're used to writing academic monographs on psychosocial problems. And now you want to switch gears for a while, and pen some whimsical piece about your daughter's first day of school. Clearly, your old style is going to pose some difficulties: "Upon arrival, Katie discerned a crowd of youngsters, of approximately her own age, size, and ethnicity, interactively engaged in rituals of acquaintanceship and familiarization, causing the subject (Katie) to respond in an immediate and

predictably affective manner (i.e., crying)." Enough said.
Your style has to be adjusted to fit your subject matter—and
your target audience.

Which is why a working writer has to change his color as
often as a chameleon. (See Rule 83, for the weariness of animal
similes.) No, you can't be what you're not—a scholar can't turn
himself into a comedian overnight—but you can modify your
voice so it's accommodated to its surroundings. For instance, the
very last thing I do before writing a magazine piece
is this: I read the magazine I'm planning to write for. If I'm
writing what I hope is an op-ed piece for the *Los Angeles Times*,
I scan that paper's editorial page. If I'm writing for *Cosmopolitan*,
I read *Cosmopolitan* (though not in a public place). In other words,
I dip myself in the pool I hope to swim in. I get used to the feel
of it, so that my own writing—even though it carries, inevitably,
my own distinctive style—will be similar enough to fit in.

Most writers know enough, instinctively, to do that. It comes
from switching back and forth from one project to another,
and from one market to another. And far from being debilitating, it's really kind of enjoyable. Instead of turning out the
same old stuff, in the same old style, it gives you a chance, and
a challenge, to try something new. You wind up finding new
colors in your palette. When your writing starts to feel too
formulaic even to you, consider a trip to some foreign locale—
a magazine you've never approached, or a form you've never
attempted. Writing a short story when you've been doing
nothing but articles, or a poem when you've been churning
out exclusively prose, is like working out a muscle you didn't
even know you had. In the end, you get what everyone wants:
a more uniformly toned and attractive body of work.

RULE 77.
Tone It Up.

If style is the symphony, then **tone is the conductor.**

Just as a conductor shapes the music to his own attitude and inclinations, so your tone dictates the thrust and the import of your own work. And your tone, the way you perceive the world you're writing about (the subject you're investigating, the characters you've created, the ideas you're exploring), tells your readers how they, too, are supposed to come away feeling. Do you feel the scorn of a Voltaire … or the all-embracing love of a Kahlil Gibran? Are you amused, bemused, or utterly unamused? Are you sitting in judgment, or just sitting?

Tone is like the dark matter of the universe: It's everywhere, but you can't ever see it. It's there in every word choice you make. Look at the difference between saying someone "waited" and someone "loitered" at the theater entrance. In the first, I'd say you were neutral; in the second, I'd say you were unfavorably disposed. And if you said that someone was "lurking" there, I'd say you were ready to call the cops.

Same event, almost the same sentence, but three very different tones, and all based on the selection of one little word. Multiply that a thousandfold, and you see how tone pervades everything.

Writers approach their work with, first, a general worldview, ranging from "this is the best of all possible worlds" all the way to "we are born between ordure and lust, and live out our days in a brimming cesspool" (this last guy should probably seek counseling). And they also have a more *specific* attitude, one that's geared to the particular job at hand. Maybe it's an editorial on gun control, and the writer wants to convey his personal indignation at not being able to own weapons of mass destruction without lily-livered liberals caterwauling about the dangers of leaving warheads in reach of small children. Well, the tone of that piece virtually dictates itself—anger and condescension, nicely mixed, and served cold.

If it's some kind of fiction, your tone gets more subtly expressed, in the way, for instance, that you describe the world your characters inhabit. F. Scott Fitzgerald wrote as if he were at once a part, and not a part, of the moneyed, insulated class; he stood, like his character Nick Carraway, to one side, and his tone was often wistful and removed. Evelyn Waugh had a wry contempt and derisory sense of humor and pinned his subjects to the walls of Oxford, Mayfair, and Brideshead. Jane Austen took the tone of a detached observer, but one to whom asperity and insight were unavoidable. Reading the work of these authors, you come away with not just a story but a perspective, a skewed version of *reality* (whatever reality is) according to the author's lights.

In your own work, all you can do is be conscious of how your own prejudices, inclinations, and ideas are influencing your tone … and then judge for yourself if you're using a sledgehammer when a ball-peen hammer would do the trick. Any tone is allowed, but the right one is often as hard to hit as a carpet tack.

Make

The only thing more perilous than explaining a joke is encouraging one.

So I am proceeding here with extreme caution.

When I say that humor is a great addition to most any piece, I mean humor that's actually, well … funny. Words so amusing that they will bring out a laugh, or at least a smile. Lines someone might want to call up a friend and quote. A turn of phrase, or a witty remark—something that surprises your readers and catches them off-guard, the way a good punch line does.

If you can come up with such stuff, you are among the blessed. (And you should quickly come out to L.A., where you can get filthy rich writing jokes for network sitcoms. God knows they could use the help.) Humor is that intangible, ineffable thing that can make even the most unpalatable gruel go down; it's the leavening agent that can lighten up even the heaviest material. In fact, the heavier the material, the more an occasional injection of levity is needed; if you can find the element of the absurd, or the note of "black humor," in subjects that are otherwise bleak, dreary, or uninviting, you'll have gone a very long way toward engaging your readers and helping them through.

The reason I'm hemming and hawing a bit here is because I've already seen way too many books and articles that claim they can teach "anyone—and we mean anyone—to be funny!" They've actually reduced jokes and humor to weird formulae— "Set up your subject, then seek to deflate it by invoking its opposite" (huh?)—or by invoking lists of words that are, supposedly, just plain funny all the time. I'm not lying when I say that I once read a piece recommending you turn to "pickle" as the fail-safe funny word. Plug it into virtually any sentence or context and it's guaranteed to provoke a "laff riot."

Some people, as you've no doubt noticed by now, are funny by nature; it's something to do with the way they look at the world and at themselves. Their "take" on things is somewhat askew, or off-kilter. But there's just no dissecting a sense of humor; it dies on the lab table. And if it just doesn't happen to be in you, there's also no way of replicating it. That's why I've been so reluctant to insist on it. If you are funny, then be funny; your readers will love you for it. The world can always use another laugh.

But if you're not funny, that's okay, too; you don't have to be. Millions of very fine people lack the humor gene. And there's nothing more painful than watching someone straining, against all odds and personal inclinations, to be funny. It defeats the whole purpose of the exercise. "Flop sweat," as nightclub comics call it, can show up on the page just as easily as on the stage, and it'll leave your readers, like any audience, restive, uncomfortable, and signaling for the check.

Writers can be a prickly lot, and nothing makes them pricklier than an editor.

It's just in the nature of the relationship.

Once you've gone through all the torment of writing, rewriting, and submitting something, whether it's a novel or a magazine piece, all you really want to hear (let's be honest about this) is unmitigated praise. You want the editor to snap it up, put through for immediate payment, and send you a box of chocolates.

And maybe that does happen, now and then—but it sure ain't the usual course of business.

Once your work has been accepted for publication, you're going to hear back from an editor—and, more than likely, it will be the same editor who has chosen your work in the first place. So that's a good thing; you should be predisposed to like this person, or at least to admire her taste in prose.

But she also has a job to do, and doing that job means telling you what, in her professional opinion, needs work. No matter how complimentary her remarks may be at the start, eventually they are going to move from all the good stuff to some of the bad. She's going to point out some flaws in your argument, or some baggy spots in your story; some language that fails to persuade, or some scenes that don't fly.

And if you react as most professional writers do, writers who take their craft seriously and have spent years honing it to a fine edge, you will scream bloody murder.

We know our work isn't perfect—but we don't believe it.

Even after all these years, it's still a shock to me that my manuscripts aren't camera-ready just as they are. In fact, I just received, from the *Los Angeles Times*, an edited version of my upcoming essay, which now begins with what I regarded as my third paragraph. The first two are missing altogether. But guess what? Upon cold and grudging reflection, I can see that the piece didn't need those two paragraphs; now it starts with a declaration, rather than a mumble. It's also shed a few other paragraphs, like unwanted pounds, later in the piece—and it's leaner and meaner as a result.

Though at times it may not feel that way, editors really do have your best interests at heart. Not because they love you so much, but because your best interests and theirs neatly overlap. A book that gets bad reviews, or an article that draws negative letters to the editor, makes trouble for both of you. If you don't look good (to paraphrase the old Vidal Sassoon slogan), the editor doesn't look good. Her responsibilities are not only to you but, in the case of journalism, to the newspaper or magazine she works for. She has to make sure that your work, no matter how unique, also conforms to all of the publication's own criteria. Does it suit their style? Is it their usual length? How does it fit into the issue or edition it's destined for? Will it work for their audience in its present state, or does it need tweaking? While you're your own boss, she might have dozens.

Which is why it behooves you to (a) squelch that scream, (b) listen carefully to what she's got to say, and (c) cooperate to the best of your abilities. I know so many would-be writers who have simply burned too many bridges by refusing to budge or by squabbling over every edit. No, I'm not suggesting that you roll over and let your precious prose be steamrollered. But you must recognize, hard as it sometimes seems, that the edited draft *may be* an improvement over the original, that the editor may know a thing or two after all, and that sometimes the most important thing is to see the present piece into print. That way, other pieces may successfully follow. An editor who isn't afraid to work with you can be the best friend you've ever had.

Did you ever listen to the Watergate tapes?
(You can hear some of them, oddly enough,
at the Richard Nixon museum in Yorba Linda,
California.) What strikes you, if you do, isn't the substance
of the conversations—much of the time, it's almost impossible
to follow—but the way that Nixon and his cronies communicate with each other. They speak in broken sentences, elliptical
phrases, grunts, vague allusions, offhanded references, bits
and pieces of what seem to be random notions and ideas.

But here's the weird part—those guys are following each
other perfectly well. Despite the fact that they talk over each
other, seldom complete a thought, interrupt, digress, and
evade, they are having what they consider to be an absolutely
ordinary discussion. And it's working for them.

But if you were to quote dialogue like this, verbatim, in
an article, your editor would figure you had lost your mind.
She would expect you to do what we have grown to consider
the unthinkable. She would expect you to edit the quotes.

Edit the quotes! you might say. Isn't that a hanging offense?

Not really. Journalists do it all the time, though we consider
it more a matter of *cleaning up*, or even *massaging*, the quotes. As
any reporter with a tape recorder can tell you, people only say
what they mean in the most roundabout way. They use thirty
words to say what they meant to convey in ten. They start one
sentence—get distracted—then start another—then return,

before they completely forget to finish the first. And they don't always choose their words with much precision. Sometimes, for the reporter, it's a matter of divining their meaning—what they *intended* to say—from the words they actually did utter. What counts, above all, is staying true to the gist and the import of their words. If, after the quote has been cleaned up and rendered halfway grammatical, it says what the subject was trying to express, then the reporter has done his job and acquitted himself in a professional manner. The idea is to stay close to the idiom in which the person normally speaks.

But what if the subject is a little rough around the edges, someone who doesn't speak the King's English? Again, you'd be wise to make the quotes hew to the general manner in which he comports himself. I remember once interviewing a crusty old farmer—he ran a date farm in the desert near Palm Springs—as part of a travel article, and when I asked him if his wife liked dates, he shook his head and said, "Nah—she got no use for the dang things." But when the article had been edited and appeared in the magazine, the farmer had suddenly become, I guess, the Secretary of Agriculture, because his answer to the question now was, "No, she doesn't enjoy dates." (Now *that*, my friends, is bad editing, and I doubt even the farmer recognized himself anymore.)

A good quote is one where your readers get the exact words, or enough of them, to understand the meaning and the tenor of your subject's remarks, and where even the subject believes that it's just what he said, and just the way he said it.

When it comes to dialogue, what's true for journalism is also true for fiction.

If you tried to emulate everyday speech *exactly*—the way Nixon and his pals, for instance, used it—then you, too, would be scrambling your characters' thoughts all over the page and leaving the reader to sort through the mess and extract some meaning.

But that's not what you do—and it's not what readers expect. When you write dialogue, you are re-creating the sound and the spirit and the shape of a verbal exchange, but you are automatically editing and refining it. You are focusing on the substance of the conversation and bringing it out in a far less discursive, and far more defined, manner. A good writer is able to convey the natural rhythms of speech without putting down every *uh* and *well* and *oh*, and without violating the vocabulary, or the integrity, of the character who is speaking. (You want your blunt old farmer to sound like a blunt old farmer.)

In fiction, dialogue has a whole range of purposes, most notably delineating your characters. Forget "you are what you eat"—"you are what you *say*" should be the fiction writer's mantra. Characters reveal themselves with every word they do, or do not, utter. And that's why the words of dialogue you choose to share with your readers are so important; each one is a clue to your character's attitudes and identity. Your dialogue should sound as immediate and unpremeditated as real speech, without all the boring stuff that usually smothers it.

Dialogue in a fictional context also has to move the story along—we have to learn something new, something potentially important, from each line or exchange. The reader assumes that's why the lines are there. You've promised a story, after all, not a transcript.

Nor did you promise to faithfully record every odd pronunciation or abbreviation common to some character's dialect. Writing in dialect, which many aspiring writers attempt, is in most cases a formula for disaster. Mark Twain could do it, but even he would have trouble getting it past an editor today— and not only because it's now considered politically incorrect. Dialect makes readers work harder than they generally want to work, and for the writer it's damnably difficult to get it on the page with any reliability. If this dialect angle is really important to you, just throw in a word or two, here and there, and leave it to the reader to supply, in his own head, the rest of the performance.

Finally, you might try a little drill I learned working in TV. Reading from the script, you were supposed to put your finger over the name of the character speaking and then try to guess whose line it was. If you couldn't do it, then the line probably needed to be rewritten, in order to be more distinctive and more in keeping with the character who was supposed to say it. (Of course, most of the shows I worked on *had* no characters.) But you might try this technique with your own fiction: Are the people speaking immediately identifiable? Or do they need a little more voice work before they fully come into themselves?

Beware of Easy Inspiration

It was a TV scene
I was particularly proud of writing.
A deranged man, afraid of supernatural
forces, retreats to his room and feverishly papers the
walls and windows with pages of the Bible.

The show's producers liked it, too. In fact, they told
me they liked it when they first saw it, years before, in *The Omen*.

Which was when I, too, remembered seeing it there. Oops.

I should have guessed something was wrong when I wrote it—
the scene came flying off my keyboard way too easily. I seldom
get an idea that good so effortlessly, and script scenes aren't
often that fully realized in my mind. Writing that scene,
I'd felt like I was totally in the zone.

**And I guess I was in the zone. Only who
knew it was someone else's?**

We are all repositories of vast amounts of information, and a lot of that information is from
books we've read, movies we've seen, stories we've
enjoyed. We've absorbed it all, and when we write,
some of it gets reprocessed. Of course, if it isn't

reprocessed enough, it's called plagiarism. But if it is, it simply serves as a kind of fuel for our own imagination and the stories we then make up on our own.

But a warning bell should go off in our heads when something comes *too* swiftly. Yes, it might just be the fruits of a sudden inspiration ... or it could be that we've accessed something we've already seen or read elsewhere. It could also be that what we've just written is a cliché, something so hackneyed and predictable that we wrote it with all the haste that countless others have written before us. Sure it came easy—we didn't have to stop to do any thinking.

I once worked under a TV head writer who claimed you should throw away your first three versions of every scene so you could then get to that fourth, and truly original, version you still had harboring inside you. Now, that man was an idiot, and as far as I could tell, he should have been throwing away his fourth, fifth, and sixth drafts, too. But there was a kernel of truth in what he said. That first draft of anything you write is often filled with easy beats, with the stuff that seems to spring, like Athena, full-blown from your brow. If a scene, a passage, a paragraph did come to you with that kind of expedience, you might want to take a second look. I'm reminded of Samuel Johnson's oft-quoted, but dead-on, warning: "What is written without effort is in general read without pleasure."

RULE 83.
Add a Dash of Metaphor.

Somewhere in our youth, we were all taught the inestimable value of metaphors and similes. If we weren't stuck in church, hearing about how "A mighty fortress is our God," we were in school learning that the "quality of mercy … droppeth like the gentle rain from heaven." If we weren't with Wordsworth as he wandered "lonely as a cloud," we were discovering that dreams deferred dried up "like a raisin in the sun." No great writers—and that went double for poets—could go very long without comparing one thing to another, without holding up the metaphorical lantern to reveal some deeper significance in the ordinary or, conversely, something mundane in the cosmic. Metaphor can inflate or deflate. It can bring something down to earth and show it to us in a human dimension, or it can toss that thing toward the sky and show us how much bigger, and more meaningful, it is than we first thought.

It's like a telescope (to use a simile): Look through one end and things get smaller; look through the other and they get larger. Either way, you've got a new perspective.

That's what makes metaphor in general such a useful tool. You don't have to find plain, blunt, unmusical words to elaborate on something; you don't have to resort to explaining things like you're writing a computer manual. Instead, you can find colorful comparisons, or surprising equivalents, that wake up your readers, make them think, and reveal what they're looking at in a whole new light. Done right, a good metaphor can accomplish all that.

But done wrong, and that's what happens all too often—the metaphor can tangle up your prose, and your thoughts, in a fine web of confusion. (I think there's a metaphor in there.) Instead of shedding light, it casts a shadow, making something less clear and comprehensible. For instance, you might easily compare a teeming railway station to an ant colony—people would get it right away—but if you compared it to an overloaded library shelf, you'd probably have more readers scratching their heads in confusion than nodding them in agreement.

Beware of animals, by the way; they'll get you into trouble. Almost any common phrase you can think of that has an animal in it is both a metaphor and a cliché. (Two for the price of one!) No character in your work should ever be as happy as a clam, as sly as a fox, as greedy as a pig, as busy as a bee, as stubborn as a mule, as quiet as a mouse; nobody should ever eat like a bird, drink like a fish, stop like a deer caught in the headlights, or run around like a chicken with its head cut off. These are all as old as Aesop and have just about as much life left in them.

There are those who have **a gift for metaphor** and those who don't (including me). **If you've got it, flaunt it;** metaphor can enrich and invigorate anything from an editorial to an epic poem.

If you haven't got it, proceed with caution.
Your words could wind up sounding as flat as a pancake.

Rid Yourself of Writing Words.

I hate readings.

Authors are generally terrible orators. They speak inaudibly; they get their own prose rhythms wrong; they're afraid to make eye contact. And that's only the half of it.

The real reason I hate readings is because most written words were never intended to be recited or performed. They were composed for the page, designed to accommodate, and even exploit, the peculiar but intimate communion that exists between the writer and his reader. They were crafted to echo in a head, not a lecture hall or meeting room.

Even the best writing—Doctorow's, Nabokov's, Bellow's— writing that gives the language a thorough workout, doesn't often sound right when read out loud. In fact, I'd venture to say, it often sounds *more* wrong than cheaper prose does. Since we're not used to hearing such carefully wrought words recited, they assume a heightened artificiality. No matter how beautiful- ly they adorn the page, or ring in our inner ear, at a reading they come off like somebody showing up at a clambake in wing tips and blazer.

Lesser prose … well, it may make for easier listening, but it's also less memorable.

Furthermore, much of it is filled with words like furthermore—

words that are written all the time but seldom spoken.

Add to that list things like *insofar, inasmuch, all told, nevertheless, nonetheless, hereafter, in future, moreover, with respect to, in terms of, at this point,* and *on the basis of.* Just about any preposition or conjunction that has to mush together two or three words to do its job is a mush you don't need. Try a simple *since,* or *when,* or *to,* or *about,* or *if;* it'll usually get you where you need to go with a lot less trouble. While you're at it, use *the former* and *the latter* sparingly. Why make your reader stop and back up? Writing is a shark—it must keep moving forward.

Knock off the "stand-in words," too. Say you're writing a piece about a swamp, but you don't want to say swamp again, so the next time you write "marsh" instead, and "bayou" the next, and "a silt-filled squishy morass" after that. Before you know it, you're up to your waist in mud, and the reader is trying to clamber out as desperately as you are.

Finally, avoid, abjure, and abstain from the editorial *we.* When *we* opine, *we* had better be standing on a soapbox, delivering a speech on world peace. And even then, we run the risk of getting hit with a well-aimed, and well-deserved, tomato. *We* used to be reserved for royals, and as far as I'm concerned, they can keep it. If you're not a king or queen, think twice.

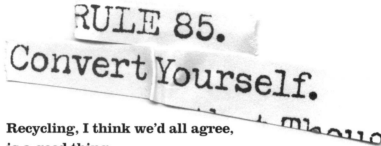

RULE 85.
Convert Yourself.

Recycling, I think we'd all agree, is a good thing.

If you write a piece of journalism, and you're able to sell it three or four times, more power to you. That's why things like First North American serial rights, secondary rights, foreign rights, etc., were invented.

But the raw material from which you write can also be recycled—and often is. That newspaper piece you wrote may contain the kernel of what could make a perfectly good short story. That short story might have the potential to be turned into a full-length novel. That novel may have such a strong, simple narrative line that it begs to be turned into a movie script. The subjects that have captured your imagination in the past are very likely to maintain their hold for some time afterward, and they may display a different, or even greater, power when expressed in a new medium.

But only if you can get out of your own way.

Since I have tended, lately, to go back and forth between scripts and books, I've had several friends ask for advice about the conversion process. They've written a novel they can't get published, or a screenplay they can't get produced, and now they want to take the story and recast it in another format. I see the logic, and I understand the impetus. I've been there myself. You've put all this energy into constructing a complete story, with a beginning, a middle, and an end, and you can't stand to let it all go to waste. It wasn't easy to get this far!

But if you find yourself in a similar situation, the first thing you have to do is take the original version of the story (whatever it is), read through it one more time, and then put it away. Put it in the bottom drawer of your desk, then close the drawer, and leave it closed.

What you remember of the story is all you need.

You'll be tempted, I know, to keep opening that drawer, but every time you do, you will be pulled back into the previous version and the story will never make a new life for itself in a fresh format. You'll make yourself crazy trying to find ways to replicate its every beat, every line of dialogue, every turn of phrase—and it cannot be done.

It cannot be done because a novel is not a movie, a movie is not a play, a play is not a short story. Every form has its own limitations and its own advantages—a novelist gets to use internal monologues, a screenwriter gets to skip long descriptions— and no story can survive intact the conversion from one form to the other. (Surely you've noticed how many good books make lousy movies.) What you have to do is re-imagine the core material, and the only way to do that is by putting the first version out of sight and out of reach. That way, the new form you're working in will have a chance of revealing to you all kinds of stuff that had never occurred to you the first time around, all kinds of opportunities for drama, humor, and suspense that either weren't there before or that you couldn't access because of the format you were working in. (In a first-person story, for instance, you can't mention that the killer just flitted, unseen, past the window—your hero didn't see it, so the reader can't either—but in a movie it's a natural, and you've just ratcheted up the audience's sense of danger without yet alerting your protagonist. It's one of the oldest tricks in the screenwriter's playbook.)

Converting a narrative is not a process of **close transcription**, it's a process of **rediscovery.** So put the original away, and **create** a whole **new version.**

RULE 86.
Punctuate That Thought.

I once had a private writing student, an honors graduate of a prestigious, small college, and I'll never forget the look on his face when I returned a chapter of his novel to him with the punctuation corrected.

A lot of the punctuation corrected.

"Yeah, okay," he said, glancing at all the little red marks. "Whatever." He shrugged and gave me the look you might give a hopeless pedant. "Don't the publishers have people who worry about this stuff?"

He was certain the book would be published very soon (even though this was only the second chapter), and when I tried to explain that this "little stuff" could keep it from getting that far, he looked at me as if I'd truly lost my mind. For him, punctuation was a trifling matter, and he certainly didn't want to waste any of our weekly conference time on it.

Frankly, neither did I. I was hoping he'd learned all this stuff back in high school, but as it appeared he had not, I had to give him a crash course in punctuation, and even more importantly, I had to explain why it *did* matter.

For one thing, errors in punctuation can quickly persuade editors you're not a professional, and that's often all the excuse they need to toss your manuscript into the wastebasket.

For another, punctuation is such a critical tool that any writer who ignores it is nuts. It's like a chef deciding to cook without pots, an artist deciding to forgo his brushes, a carpenter tossing out his hammer and nails. It's an essential part of what you have to work with, and it's not a hindrance, it's a help.

Dashes and hyphens, ellipses and semicolons, periods and parentheses—they seem, I know, like so many niggling little details (that's certainly what my writing student thought), but in fact they're the means to inject inflection and expression into your work. You can't *raise* your voice on paper, not literally, but an exclamation mark can make your intentions plain. You can't *lower* your voice on paper, not literally, but a parenthetical phrase allows you to slip in a sotto voce aside. A dash can do exactly what its name implies—pull your reader brusquely long— and a colon can bring him to a sudden stop. Commas, which seem to fall in and out of good repute, are like traffic cones on a highway, guiding your reader this way and that, around obstacles, into the next lane. Personally, I love commas (which may be evident in this book) because I want my readers to hear the words exactly the way I do, in the same cadence I first imagined them.

But to my mind, you, the writer, remain the higher authority—and if you want to bend the rules of punctuation to suit your own purpose, to make the meaning of your work more clear or the rhythm more engaging, then go right ahead. That's actually what those pesky little marks were invented for— to help you make your writing voice as distinctive as possible. Think about them carefully, and use them freely, to convey the music of your prose as precisely and as beautifully as you can.

Build the Perfect Reader.
RULE 87.

In many ways, building your perfect reader is like training a dog.

For good behavior, like sitting still and paying attention, you offer rewards. For bad conduct—failing to turn the page, turning on the TV—you have to corral the wayward beast and once again regain his trust. A loyal reader is a writer's best friend.

But, to an extent seldom acknowledged, such readers have to be built from the ground up. Only with constant positive reinforcement and regular treats will your readers become, and remain, who you need them to be.

First of all, you have to grab them. If your opening pages, or even your opening paragraphs, don't contain something striking or memorable, you may have lost your only chance of snagging them. It's a multichannel world we live in, and the mental remote is always in play.

In those same early passages, you must also give your readers a clear sense of what they're about to encounter. If you start out with a high-minded paean to democracy, they settle down in their chairs with their thinking caps on, prepared to absorb a valuable lesson in civics. If you begin with a casual anecdote about kids and car travel, then they're already primed for some smiles. The bait-and-switch technique, so beloved by car dealers, seldom works with prose—readers catch on quickly and leave with alacrity. (After all, no one's watching.)

But readers respond to the writer even more than to the subject matter. If you start out with the right tone of voice—

engaging, direct, clever—you can persuade them to come along for a ride they would never otherwise have taken. (I just read a long article about a rock-and-roll roadie that captured me, against my better judgment, with its opening description of the guy's multiple tattoos.) If you're using humor (see Rule 78 for the Olympian overview), then use it quickly—why not let your audience know right off the bat that they're in for a few laughs? But don't go to town. The best comedians know when to let the audience breathe for a few seconds; they know they have to spend a little time setting up the next big laugh.

Know, too, how to leave your audience. No, they don't have to be laughing (though that can be a good thing), but they do have to feel satisfied, rewarded. The ending of the article, essay, book, whatever, has to give them the sense that they've completed the journey and have landed comfortably and intact. If they signed on for a luxury cruise, you don't want to heave them onto the wharf with a bad case of dysentery and a bump on the head.

Above all, love your readers, and they'll love you back. If you write in cringing fear, waiting for the critical brickbats, then your fear, and your resentment, will come through in the work. But if you write with an amiable, fearless disposition— blithely confident of a fine reception—your own attitude will infect your readers. Do this enough, and you will eventually achieve what all of us who write most covet: an audience already attuned to us and our work, ready to laugh at our jokes, nod at our solemnities and, best of all, log on to Amazon and buy our collected works.

RULE 88.

Pass the Scalpel.

Okay, let's say you've just finished reading something really terrific. A magazine piece so engrossing that you missed your bus stop, an essay that touched you more deeply than you would ever have expected, a book you can't stop thinking about, long after you turned the last page.

Instead of just moving on, picking up something new to read, or doing something else entirely, stop. Take that article, that essay, that book, and lay it out, as if on a lab table, for a lesson in gross anatomy. You can't call it a postmortem—the thing is still alive—but you could call it a postreadem. Your goal? To figure out what the writer did to make his work such an affecting experience for you.

The first time through, you were caught up in the work, just letting it unfold and carry you along. But that's not what you're doing now. Now you're looking at it with a cold, critical eye. You're looking for the secrets of its success. I think the first time I ever did this was when I was around ten years old, and I had just finished reading a James Bond novel (*The Man with the Golden Gun*, if memory serves). The climax had been painstakingly drawn out, and my preteen mind had been riveted for page after page. How, I wondered, had Ian Fleming pulled it off? Looking back over the last chapter or two, I saw that he'd cut away from the main action, gone off on another tangent for a few pages or paragraphs, and then returned again to the big chase. Just when you thought Bond's number was up, Fleming would divert your attention, and when you finally got back, something unexpected would happen to keep the drama cooking.

I tried it several times thereafter in my own stories, with varying degrees of success. But I never forgot the lesson.

Good writing achieves its effects almost invisibly; you don't see the strings, and you don't see them being pulled. Unless, of course, you look, and look hard. Ask yourself, *How did this essayist manage to draw me in so powerfully?* Did she reveal herself so honestly that you were irresistibly intrigued? How did she tell her story, or make her points, so effortlessly that you felt the power and the truth of what she had to say? How did the book you were just reading use its shifting points of view to such advantage? (You should see my copy of a Scott Spencer novel, *Men in Black*, sometime—I couldn't believe how he'd managed to go back and forth between first person and third, in alternating chapters, and until I started diagramming the book, I hadn't even thought you were *allowed* to do that. I thought a committee of English teachers would descend on your house and arrest you.)

Wordsworth wrote that "We murder to dissect," and the guy had a point. But sometimes it's worth it. When you take apart and analyze a successful piece of writing, you get to see how the thing was put together and why it worked its magic on you so well. If you're lucky, you'll also be able to capture some of that same magic in your own little bottle someday.

Gather Ye Moonbeams!
RULE 89.

Want to know how to pick out the born writer in a grammar school classroom **?**

Look for the kid staring out the window, lost in space.

Writers are born daydreamers. It's not that we can't focus—we have to be able to do that in order to get any writing done—but our normal default state, the condition to which we will inevitably return, is one of unfettered free association. Our thoughts, ungoverned, lead us in all sorts of directions, and we willingly follow. John Fowles once remarked that "in a novelist, a wandering mind is a good thing."

Some of our best ideas come to us in those aimless reveries, things the logical mind would never have put together. The trick is catching these ephemeral notions, like butterflies in our net, before they flit away.

That's why many writers I know make a practice of getting out of bed, throwing some cold water on their face, and then immediately sitting down to work. They want to catch the loose, unedited, free-ranging liberty of the dream state. They want to hear only one voice in their head—their own true voice—without the distraction and the clamor the rest of the day is sure to bring. Freud said, "Dreams are the royal road to the unconscious," and whatever you may think about stuff like his notion of penis envy, he was right about this. If you can write before you've lost all contact with your dreaming self, you may find a whole trunkload of material you would never otherwise have opened.

But maybe you're like me. Maybe you get out of bed only when and if the mattress has actually caught fire. And maybe you have to have the radio blasting Bob Seger & the Silver Bullet Band just to find your way to the shower. Maybe the dog needs—and I mean *needs*—to be walked first thing. For you, like me, this morning routine may never get off the ground.

So try my alternative. Around my house, at about nine o'clock at night, the phone stops ringing, the garbage trucks are no longer rumbling through the alleyway, and the doorbell isn't being buzzed. Things settle down, and I settle down with them. Instead of catching the dream state after waking up, I catch it before going to sleep. If I'm at loose ends, with nothing much in the works, I let my thoughts roam.

Writers are always getting accused of sitting around and doing nothing, when in fact doing nothing—or what *looks* like it—is useful and even necessary. (My wife used to catch me at it and say, "Are you brooding again?" and only after I'd insisted, for the tenth time, that I wasn't brooding but *thinking* did she learn to tiptoe around me at those times.) If I'm in the middle of some project, I nudge my mind in that general direction, and when I've finally gotten into the mood, and hit upon what I want to write next, I plunk myself down in front of the computer and go at it. Depending on your own sleep schedule, you might get in a good two or three hours of work before having a midnight snack and calling it a day, or night, as the case may be.

RULE 90. Lose Your Perspective.

Years ago, when I was reviewing books, I was assigned a fat novel called *Weaveworld*, by Clive Barker—an immensely complicated story, it turned out, about a whole world of tiny creatures hidden in the fabric and pattern of a carpet.

And although my first reaction was, *What is this guy smoking?*, I soon found myself immersed in the tale and enjoying every minute of it.

What Barker, one of the most imaginative writers I've ever encountered, was able to do was draw me into that microworld and keep me there. And he was able to do it because he believed in it so passionately himself. Barker, whose body of work covers a vast range from flat-out horror to far-out fantasy, loses himself in the worlds he creates, and makes them so palpable, his readers can lose themselves there, too.

When you write, as Barker does, any work of speculative fiction, you must somehow contrive to forget about all normal constraints and let the story lead you. You have to stop telling yourself, *This couldn't happen*, or, *That never does*, and instead open yourself up to all the possibilities. It's no harder to type something fantastic than it is to type something ordinary.

And the experience can prove tremendously liberating. When a piece of work is going well, you're immersed in the world of your own creating, you're lost in a universe where you are God and you can make up pretty much any rules you want. Time flows backward? *Fine*. There are five sexes? *Okay*. Animals talk? *Gotcha*. If you don't bury yourself up to your eyeballs in that world, you won't be able to write about it with any conviction or construct it with any solidity.

And yet, for most writers, there's always that little voice in the back of the head saying, *Are you crazy? Who's going to believe in something this strange?* (such as a whole universe embedded in an old rug). *Have you lost all perspective?*

No, what you've done is gain it—a new one, one that allows you to see a world where none existed, to tailor it to your own specifications and function within its imaginary parameters. The only way to find such a place is to lose yourself there.

RULE 91.

Take Up Whittling.

Most writers, when asked what they like to do in their spare time, first say reading,

followed by some after thoughts, like going to the movies,
riding a bike, taking long romantic walks on the beach at sunset.

Usually, they're lying about everything but the reading.

Many writers, and I'm one of them, live in their heads. If you asked us why we even had bodies, we'd say it was so that we had something to carry our heads around. (Once, I visited a local gym, and when I didn't sign up, the salesman called me up the next week and said, "This is Brad, the voice of your conscience." "First of all," I told him, "I don't have a conscience, and if I did, it wouldn't be named Brad." Nor did I sign up.)

Some writers—and this mystifies even me—like to spend their spare time doing crossword puzzles or playing Scrabble. To me, those things seem much too much like work. Sitting in a chair, moving words and letters around, *for fun*? No way.

But I do recognize the importance of finding an outlet, a hobby, something to distract you from the toil of writing.

Many options present themselves—bungee jumping, Alpine mountaineering, spelunking—and all of them are fine choices, expressly because they don't involve words. (Bungee jumping may involve the occasional scream, but I don't think that counts.)

What you need is a real holiday—not a busman's holiday—from the work you've been doing. If strenuous physical activity is as repugnant to you as it is to me, then you might try to find some other mindless, even monotonous, activity to indulge in: knitting, stamp collecting, whittling bars of laundry soap into perfect representations of your favorite classical composers. Winston Churchill made a hobby of bricklaying. The goal is simply to break the spell of words, if only for a few hours, that often holds writers in its grasp. You want your hands to be busy with something other than a pen or a keyboard—what better way to ward off carpal tunnel syndrome? And you want your thoughts— at least your conscious thoughts—to be focused on something other than the opening salvos of your editorial or the dramatic conclusion of your play. Throw yourself into gourmet cooking, and you'll even be able to get dinner ready at the same time.

RULE 92.
Save Every Scrap.

In the old days,
before computers, it was a lot easier to hang on to your drafts.
For one thing, typing was such a chore, comparatively speaking,
that you were loath to toss out anything you had labored over.
You were also, sometimes, reluctant to make the small changes
the piece really required; who wanted to type a whole page all
over again just to drop one clumsy passage? These days, you
just highlight whatever you don't like, hit Delete, and it's gone.

But most writers I know don't do that. Most of us either
save those words we cut in a file somewhere, or we print them
out and stuff them in a drawer—where, chances are, they will
molder into dust. So why bother? For a host of reasons, only
one of which I think is really valid.

Some writers believe in saving every word they write because
they believe these words could come in handy later. Maybe
they'll go back to a section of the piece, realize they should never
have taken out the stuff they did, and be delighted to find that
they can now just reinsert it. Waste not, want not.

There's also the chance that something they've edited out
of one piece will work, later on, in something else altogether.
A scene that doesn't play in one story may provide the jumping-
off point for another; an argument that doesn't quite mesh with
the rest of the book it's in might make a nicely contained essay
for the *New York Times* magazine. All of it gets tossed into a file,
a drawer, a cardboard box under the desk, there to live in hope
of the final resurrection.

Which, to be honest, almost never comes.

Most of the stuff you cut stays cut, and for good reason.

It's very hard to take any portion of one manuscript and make it fit, with any success, in another. The more you try to fiddle, the more slippery and awkward the task becomes. You almost always wind up with what looks like a mannequin in an ill-fitting suit: lifeless and lacking in style. Apart, perhaps, from the inspiration provided by the original words, there's generally nothing worth saving; you are better off just taking the gist of it and making something fresh and new. (And that's assuming you still have the interest in the material to do that, which isn't always the case.)

Still, with all that said, I'll tell you the best reason for hanging on to every draft and every scrap of prose you write. And here it is: If you throw something out, irretrievably, you will wake up in the dead of night convinced that the stuff you discarded is the best work you had ever done, that it was filled with priceless material you will never again be able to re-create or re-imagine, and that you were mad not to see its extraordinary virtues at the time. You may even find yourself climbing into a Dumpster with a flashlight to try to retrieve the crumpled pages. (Ask me about that sometime.) Forget about the fact that you saw good reason to toss it at the time; now you'll think it was pure genius—unless, that is, you're again able to hold it in your hand, read it over, and say to yourself, Oh, yeah, that's why it stunk.

In my book, **there are lots of bad ways** to introduce an anecdote, but perhaps the worst is, **"This is the funniest story you've ever heard."**

Followed closely by, **"You won't believe what I'm about to tell you."**

For one thing, the story is never the funniest one I've ever heard (I tell those myself, thank you very much), and for another, I seldom believe what I'm told, anyway.

But what makes these intros so bad is that they set up expectations in the audience that will almost certainly go unfulfilled. If you start a story—either spoken or written—with a bold, over-the-top billing like that, you've raised the bar to an untenable height, and you've issued a sort of challenge to your audience. You've virtually dared them not to like what you're about to relate, and a lot of them, ornery by nature, will consequently put up some resistance. Since you told them how to react, they are now determined to react differently, just to prove they can't be pushed around.

This is not the right foot to get off on.

When you're writing, you're asking your readers to accept what you tell them. You're making a promise of sorts—that you will absorb, entertain, amuse, thrill, scare, and amaze them. Your promise is implicit in every word you write, words intended to hold their attention and keep them avidly reading.

But if you make that promise explicit—if you tell them what a great treat they're in for—then you'd better be darned sure you can back it up. If you can't, you'll have broken faith with your readers and they may decide, since they no longer trust you, to turn around and go home.

Every writer is, to some extent, a carnival barker, trying to lure the passersby into his tent. Lord knows there's a lot of stuff to read out there, and if you expect to snag someone's attention for very long, you've got to make a pretty persuasive case, and you've got to make it pretty quickly. But let the work speak for itself. Let the unfolding of your story or the seductive quality of your prose draw your readers in and, with luck, hold them there. Don't *tell* them how they're supposed to feel or react—just cast your spell so effectively that they *do* feel it.

RULE 94.
Keep Your Prose Clean.

The last thing I want to do is enter the current culture wars, especially on the conservative side of the aisle, but I do think it's worth saying a few words on the use of profanity.

First of all, using profanity, epithets, and coarse terms and/or dialogue in your work is, in my opinion, permissible and sometimes necessary.

If you're writing in a freewheeling, discursive tone of voice, swinging for the bleachers, then go for it. We're all grown-ups here. If you're writing for a publication that offers a lot of latitude and a lot of attitude to match, then, again, be my guest. If you're writing an article about prison inmates, and this happens to be the way they talk, quote freely and verbatim. If you're writing a novel about Wall Street traders, whose language, in my experience, is some of the filthiest ever uttered, show it, and them, for what it is. I've got no problem with using all the resources, and all the colors, of the language we've got. I'm not easily shocked, and neither are most readers, editors, and publishers.

But some are.

And that's why most writers err on the side of caution. It's not that they censor themselves, it's more that they maintain an awareness, however vague and inchoate, of their audience. When they write an article or essay, they keep the general public in mind. Would something they've written give offense? Would it appall a few prissy souls, or nearly everyone in the country? Is the use of the volatile stuff essential to the piece, or is it merely there for some kind of shock value or effect? And how much of it, honestly, is needed to make the point? If they're writing for a mass circulation publication, most writers will take care to remain a polite neighbor to all the other writers and articles in the issue.

As with anything, profanity loses its impact with overuse. The more a character, or a writer, swears and cusses, the more unremarkable the words become. That could be a good thing—maybe you're trying to inure your readers to a certain kind of world. But, overall, if you want to retain the curious potency of the "bad words," you have to parcel them out sparingly. That way, when you do elect to use them, they will still have the requisite power to rock your readers back on their heels, scorch the eyebrows right off their faces, or send them running for the smelling salts.

There's no place like life to go for inspiration.

RULE 95. Protect Your Inspiration.

But it's not always that easy.

How exactly do you draw on the people, the incidents, the daily rounds of your own life without possibly exposing someone else's secrets, giving offense when you never intended to or, worst of all, getting sued?

When you're writing, either fiction or non, you're pulling details, observations, thoughts from a thousand different sources, most of them rooted in reality—*your* reality. You're writing about friends and family members, you're writing about places you go, events you've attended, confrontations you've actually had. Those are the things that fill your creative well, as it were, and from which you're going to extract your article ideas, your stories, your anecdotes.

If you're writing fiction—something that loudly proclaims itself to be *made-up stuff*—you have one easy out. If someone thinks she's spotted herself in one of your characters, and in an unflattering guise, you can always flat-out deny it. "You? Of course not. Why, I was actually thinking of someone I knew years ago, back in Akron." Or, the fall-back position, "The character is a composite."

But, thankfully, this seldom happens, and for one simple reason. Most people think pretty well of themselves, and they never see themselves, as you or your narrator might, in an unfavorable light. I have a friend who's written a string of novels featuring some of the most horrendous wives imaginable, but he always covers himself by dedicating the books to his own dear spouse—who, so far at least, has failed to take umbrage, or initiate divorce proceedings.

In nonfiction, the trick is more difficult. This material is supposed to be true to life. Let's say you want to write a humor column about your Uncle Barney and his crazy get-rich-quick schemes ... but Barney, as it happens, is still alive, he's still your uncle, and you're going to have to sit next to him at Thanksgiving. You don't want to hurt the old guy's feelings, but you know this is great material. You can start, of course, by cleverly changing his name. And instead of making him your uncle, you can make him a neighbor. And instead of telling the story about his mushroom farming in the cellar, you can make up something else that never really happened. All these things may help—Uncle Barney may not see himself in this oddball neighbor of yours—but the heck of it is, *you* may not see Uncle Barney in there anymore, either. The power of the piece, which derived from the real Uncle Barney and your relationship to him, may have evaporated in the process.

This is the conundrum that's a part of every writer's life. You can make the small concessions, but the more changes you make, the further you will get, inevitably, from the power source. All you can really try to do is stay as true as possible to the core of the experience, or the real person, you're writing about. If it winds up getting you in trouble, remember that you're in good company.

The writer doesn't breathe who hasn't had to apologize to someone.

RULE 96. Magnetize Yourself

Of all the afflictions that befall writers, dithering is one of the most common. Faced with seventeen different ideas, for everything from short stories to screenplays, many writers waste tons of precious time flitting from one to the other, wondering what to fully embark upon. It's so easy to start writing a novel, then hit an obstacle, and quickly decide that the short-story idea looks much more promising after all ... until that idea, too, hits a rough patch. Then, suddenly, the stage-play idea appears in a very appealing light. And so on and so forth, until weeks have gone by, and what you've finally got in the end is nothing but a bunch of false starts, first chapters, and opening scenes.

But once you do make a decision,
and pick one project and stick to it,
you'll notice something strange happens.

(I don't know a writer who wouldn't second this.)

You become a virtual magnet for related information and ideas. Suddenly, you will start discovering, all around you, all sorts of juicy tidbits—observations, quotes, statistics, stories— that directly relate to, and nicely amplify, the project you're working on. You'll stop at a yard sale and find an old book, for fifty cents, which provides great background research. You'll turn on the radio and hear a song that's exactly what your heroine might be listening to in her big scene. You'll open the morning paper and come across a piece in the science section that neatly explains a rather arcane bit of business in your nonfiction tome.

The more you focus in on one piece of work, the more attuned you are to everything around you that might help. And there's *a lot*. Writers are scavengers—we find all kinds of odds and ends and either paste them into what we're working on, or into notebooks for later use. (I am forever finding old magazine articles and newspaper clippings that I once cut out for reasons I can now no longer remember.) But when I'm immersed in one particular project, I am consistently amazed at the things that come to hand and that seem to have been tailor-made for me. If I weren't such a skeptic, I'd say there was a kind of divine providence behind it. (But I'd hate to think that God was spending time helping me with my thriller while famine, plague, and war afflicted millions.)

Whatever the mechanism behind it, once you choose a subject (or, as the case may be, let it choose *you*), you will soon discover that the world is behind you on this, and it'll start to provide you with a plethora of helpful bits and pieces, and sometimes even answers.

Who cares where all this good stuff comes from? Just accept it and be grateful.

Spill Your
Secrets

If you like paradoxes, try these.

Want to reach the broadest public? Go private.

Want to move your readers deeply? Think only of yourself.

Want to touch a universal chord? Focus on the intensely personal.

In the struggle to reach an audience and connect with them in a powerful way, writers are forever trying to find the big topic, the big scene, the big, all-encompassing embrace. How, they wonder, can they make their own experiences more universal, how can they find a way to relate what they know and feel to what thousands, even millions of other people may think and feel? How can they forge a bond between their own limited perspective and that of all these faceless, nameless readers with whom they are, nonetheless, desperately anxious to communicate?

And the answer is simple.

It's not a matter of going wide—of trying to fill the biggest canvas or paint in the broadest strokes. You don't have to wrestle with issues of war and peace, or in fiction with characters of epic proportion. Nothing has to be of immense or shocking scale. You don't have to raise a monument.

What you do have to do is *dig*.

Deep.

The more specific you become, the more generally felt your writing will be. The more revealing you are—of your own emotions and thoughts, no matter how uncomfortable some of them may be—the more you will strike a chord in others. The more you are willing to examine yourself, honestly and openly, the more your work will speak to people you would think have nothing in common with you.

And the reason isn't so hard to come up with. We're all alike, in more ways than we'd like to admit, and we all have secrets we think no one else could possibly share—doubts and fears we think assail only us, shameful emotions and unspoken needs we're sure consume nobody else, dreams and desires we wouldn't confide even to our analysts. (Go ahead and admit it—it *killed* you when your best friend sold her book in two weeks!) We're all a bundle of neuroses and insecurities, prevarications and procrastinations, slippery evasions, broken promises, and insincere avowals. The list goes on and on, and it's not pretty.

But it is true. And that's all that matters to you. Because if you, as a writer, can tell the truth, if you can really take the elevator down to your own subbasement and then come back up with what you found there, you will never want for a responsive audience. They'll be endlessly curious, and oh so relieved to discover that there's someone else on the planet who's just as screwy as they are.

Even if
Aristotle hadn't
told us so, by now we'd
have figured out that stories
need a beginning, a middle, and an
end. And the very fact that they do means
that they're going to need a tense—a temporal
frame in which the sequence of events unfolds (E.M.
Forster's formula of "and then … and then … and then … ").

Generally, that's going to mean you'll be writing your
fiction in the past tense. You're going to be relating a story
that started some time ago—eons, or just minutes—and that
moves, through an escalating sequence of events, toward some
conclusion. That's why "Once upon a time" has been around
so long—it sets us up nicely for a straightforward, linear narrative, at the same time that it promises us a surprising journey.

But lately it's become fashionable to tell some stories in the
present tense. "Jack goes to the counter and orders a bologna
sandwich. He eats it outside. He wonders where bologna
comes from." Frankly, I find most such present-tense stories
to be about that gripping. The idea, of course, is that the
story will have a "You are there!" quality, a spontaneous,
realistic, unfolding-before-your-very-eyes feel. But of
course it's *not* unfolding right then and there—somebody
wrote it up and sent it to a publisher, and we all know that—
so I find the pretense precious and vaguely annoying.

And although you wouldn't think it, using the present tense also has a way of putting the story at a slight *remove*.

While the past tense allows us to move forward, at any pace we like, toward a future which is, in fact, our present (does that track?), the present tense roots us in the here and now. It negates the past, eliminates all but the immediate future, and slows the pace of the narrative.

Screenplays are written in the present tense, always, but that's because we're not really meant to read them; they're a series of images and scenes and lines of dialogue designed to unspool before us while we sit passively in our seats munching our vastly overpriced popcorn. As literature, screenplays hardly count; they're more like a blueprint or a business plan.

Where present tense *does* come in handy is in things like technical or science writing. You don't want to tell us where the screw *went*, you want to tell us where it *goes*. And when you're writing, say, about the behavior of subatomic particles, you're writing under the assumption that the little buggers are acting the same way, right now, as they always have and that they'll go on doing it forever. The electron didn't *spin* around the nucleus; it *spins* around it. Some things, like your prose, we assume to be eternal.

Call It Quits.

RULE 99.

Writing is all about perseverance. No question about it. It's all about dedicating yourself to the project at hand and, whatever the obstacles, seeing it through to completion.

But it's also a matter of knowing when to quit.

Sometimes you're going to have a bad idea. Or you're going to start on something that just plain doesn't work. Sometimes you're going to lay an egg.

So when is it fair—and wise—to throw in the towel on work that isn't working? Lord knows, there are lots of things militating *against* the decision. For one, you've already put in all this time and effort, writing thousands of words that will now languish in obscurity. For another, you don't want to think of yourself as a quitter. Don't all the writing books and teachers advise you not to give up, to keep on plugging? Don't they all tell you that these sloughs of despond are only natural and nothing to worry about?

True enough, but sometimes your unshakable misgivings and increasing doubts are valid; they're telling you something. What's important is to listen carefully. They're not, for instance, telling you that you're a worthless writer. They're not telling you that you're a quitter. They're not telling you that you will never write again.

They're simply telling you that this one thing, this one project, isn't going anywhere. That even you have lost interest in it for some reason. And if it's not holding your own interest any longer, how can it ever be expected to grip a reader? In two words: It can't.

There isn't a professional writer on Earth who hasn't had to abandon an essay, a poem, an article. But that didn't stop these same writers from starting on something else. Sometimes the abandoned projects serve as the necessary corrective, the false start that points the way to the true one. Sometimes they're a liberating exercise, a sneeze that had to be gotten over. And now it has.

Sometimes they're just duds. Ideas that fizzled. Soufflés that fell flat. Cars that ran out of gas. Don't be mad at them; don't be mad at yourself. Just quietly slip the clunkers out of sight, chalk 'em up to experience, and move on.

If, however, this happens over and over and over again, then it may be time to ask yourself the more important question. Do you enjoy writing? Is it really what you were meant to do? Not everyone is meant to—and there is no shame in that. Writing is a choice, and if the choice is, with depressing consistency, making you miserable, choose something else.

Reading, for instance, makes a terrific alternative.

Grant Yourself a Title.

RULE 100.

Some writers are great at titling; some (like me) stink. But if you think you can slap any old title on your work and then send it out, you're making a big mistake.

And missing a big opportunity.

Your title is the first thing an editor, a publisher, or your readers are going to see, and it tells them a lot about what's coming. If you write an article and put a silly, lighthearted title on it—"The Ten Dopiest Things You Can Say to a Girl"—it tells them they're in for a breezy (and possibly pointless) read. If you write a book with what I think of as the "high colonic" title—*The History of the World: An Eschatological Approach to the Structures of Societal Life and the Parameters of Human Endeavor*—then they know it's time to buckle their seat belts. (Colons show up in many nonfiction titles, and almost invariably in books from academic presses, where the author has to make sure the subject sounds sufficiently weighty, obscure, and intimidating.) Your title is the banner that brings customers into your store, so make it bold, colorful, clever, provocative, mysterious, controversial, funny, intriguing, *anything*—just don't make it boring.

If you have trouble coming up with a title, it may signal a deeper problem with the piece you've been working on.

Whenever I've written, say, a humorous essay (or what I think *passes* as a humorous essay), and I can't come up with any title at all that seems to fit the piece, it usually means the piece hasn't really congealed as it should have. The more I unsuccessfully cast about for a title that speaks to the point of the piece, the more I realize that maybe, just maybe, the piece doesn't *have* a single, clear point. Maybe it's grown too diffuse, or it rambles around over too much ground. What did I think was so funny in the first place?

By the same token, sometimes it helps to come up with a working title in advance. You can always change it, of course, but if you're worried about going off track or forgetting the original impetus for the piece at hand, a working title can serve as a kind of lodestone, keeping you pointed in the right direction. It can also give the work a sense of solidity in your own mind—you're not just writing any old thing, you're writing *One Man's Poison: Everything That's Wrong With the World and Why.*

Novels, screenplays, and plays are a nightmare for titling. Chances are, they're about many things—they've got characters, plots, themes (buried and blatant.) With all that to encompass, how—and what—do you fix on? And haven't all the good titles already been taken? (One of the many advantages of an Amazon.com world is that you can quickly check your title ideas against whatever is already out there.)

For inspiration, lots of writers turn to the same sources—*Bartlett's Familiar Quotations* and the Bible are probably the top two.

You're looking for short, pithy phrases and expressions—sometimes they're good just as they are, sometimes they need a little tweaking. A title with a Biblical provenance (*The Sun Also Rises*), or a poetic one (*Tender Is the Night*) lends a classy tone to any project. Looking for just that sort of thing for one of my own novels, I kept coming up empty-handed—until I decided to do some reverse engineering. I composed my own snatch of faux antique verse, credited it in the book's epigraph to an anonymous poet, then lifted the few words I needed from it to give myself a decent title.

Am I proud of this behavior? No. But I can't say I'm all that ashamed of it, either.

There are few things in this world more desperate than a writer with no title to stick on his cover.

RULE 101.

In 1968, the poet Marianne Moore was giving a reading and when she offered to field some questions, someone in her audience asked her what advice, if any, she would give to an aspiring poet "who hates words."

After thinking about it for a few seconds, Moore said, "That may be very auspicious. Words are a very great trap."

With all due respect to Marianne Moore, who won the Pulitzer and the National Book Award, that was the wrong answer! The questioner was probably just showing off—"Look at me, a poet who hates words! Is that deep or what?"—but if it was more than that, if the questioner really and truly hated words, then that's when Moore should have suggested barber school.

Writers love words, or at least the real ones do.

Oh, they may get plenty mad at them at times, the way you do at a family member who disappoints you in some way. (The worst injuries are the ones your loved ones inflict.) But words are all you have to work with, and when they don't come easily, when they don't sound on the page the way they did in your head, it can be the most frustrating thing in the world. You know what you *wanted*

Love Words.

to say, you *thought* you knew how you wanted to say it, but those darn words you've just typed are somehow missing the essence of it. So, you have to strike them out and try again.

And then, who knows? You may have to cross them out all over again after that.

Each time, you may come a little closer to what you want—to the scene you see in your mind's eye, to the argument you want to make, to the sentiment you wish to express—but the words aren't yet there. You still have to search through your toolbox for the right combination of nuts and bolts and nails to build the thing you envisioned.

And that toolbox holds every word you've managed to accumulate over the years … years of living, years of listening, and years of reading. All the words you've over-heard in supermarket lines and subway cars. All the words you've read on cereal boxes and movie posters, in comics and classics, in tabloid newspapers and classroom texts. (Writers read *everything*.) All the words you've spoken, in passion and in anger, all the words you've had thrown right back at you. If you don't love words, if you don't love what they can do and how they sound in the right combination, and the infinitesimally different shades of meaning among them, if you're not grateful as hell that you drew English as your native tongue (one of the richest, most varied, and *universally known* languages), then, like Marianne Moore's questioner, you ought to look into another line of work.

Writers wallow in words like pigs in a mud puddle, and the dirtier we get, the happier we are.

RULE - 102. Break the Rules.

The cover of the book says 101 Rules—and that's why I'm writing 102.

Just to prove that rules are made for breaking.

For example, for every writer who writes in the morning, there's one who writes only at night.

For every writer who plows ahead, never looking back, there's one who agonizes over every word and cannot go forward without polishing every syllable that has come before.

For every writer who works from an elaborate outline, there's one who flies by the seat of his pants.

Successful writers are always being quizzed. Do you write on a computer? What kind? What gave you the idea for that book or article or movie script? How long did it take you to write it? How much were you paid for it? How do you feel about reviews? Do you read the bad ones? What are you working on next? How do you get started? How do you know when you're done?

Implicit in all the questioning is the notion that there's some secret to the writing life, some way of working that professionals know—and share—and that amateurs suffer from not knowing. And the only real secret is that everything works—for somebody. Finding out what works for you is all a matter of trial and error. Are you writing the first draft of your book in longhand, on a legal pad, while sitting in a rocking chair? If it works for you (as it has for me), then that's your secret. Or, are you working on your laptop on the crowded commuter train to the office? If the work gets done, then that's all you need to know.

At every public event I do, I get asked, as most writers do, something about inspiration and about why I write. Usually I brush it off with some dumb joke about the mortgage payment being due, or by quoting that famous old saw of Samuel Johnson's: "No man but a blockhead ever wrote except for money." I even stuck that quote on one of my books, years ago, as the epigraph—and I've always regretted it. Why? Because I didn't believe it then, not really, and I don't believe it now. If I were that interested in money, I'd have listened to my parents and gotten a real job years ago.

I write, as most writers do, for other reasons. I write, frankly, because I want to be heard. I want people to take me into account and listen to what I have to say. I feel like there's a big public debate going on all the time, all around me, everywhere from the news channels to the bookstore shelves, and I simply can't bear to be left on the sidelines. Never could.

Writing is a way to enter into the permanent record everything from your transitory thoughts to your very existence, and no matter how modest a writer may claim his goals to be, on some level he's doing this for posterity. You write in the unspoken hope that you will become part of the passing parade that was your time.

As goals go, you could do a whole lot worse.

4-25-05

THE END